THE ONE PERCENTER CODE

THE ONE PERCENTER CODE

HOW TO BE AN OUTLAW IN A WORLD GONE SOFT

DAVE NICHOLS

PHOTOGRAPHY BY KIM PETERSON

motorbooks

Quarto is the authority on a wide range of topics.

Quarto educates, entertains and enriches the lives of our readers—enthusiasts and lovers of hands-on living.

www.quartoknows.com

First published in 2012 by Motorbooks, an imprint of Quarto Publishing Group USA Inc., 400 First Avenue North, Suite 400, Minneapolis, MN 55401 USA. This edition published 2016. Telephone: (612) 344-8100 Fax: (612) 344-8692

quartoknows.com
Visit our blogs at quartoknows.com

Motorbooks titles are also available at discounts in bulk quantity for industrial or sales-promotional use. For details contact the Special Sales Manager at Quarto Publishing Group USA Inc., 400 First Avenue North, Suite 400, Minneapolis, MN 55401 USA.

10 9 8 7 6 5 4 3 2 1

ISBN: 978-0-7603-5038-6

Digital edition published in 2012
eISBN: 978-1-6105-8555-2

The Library of Congress has cataloged the hardcover edition of this book as follows:

Nichols, Dave, 1954-.
  The one percenter code : how to be an outlaw in a world gone soft / Dave Nichols ; photography by Kim Peterson.
     255 p : ill. ; 23 cm.
  Includes index.
  ISBN 978-0-7603-4272-5 (hardcover)
  1. Motorcycle gangs--United States. 2. Motorcycle clubs—United States--History. 3. Motorcycling--United States. 4. Subculture. 5. Motorcycling--Social Aspects. I. Title
  HV6488.N53 2012
  364.106'603--dc23
                                    2011277902

Editor: Darwin Holmstrom
Design Manager: James Kegley
Design: John Barnett
Layout: Diana Boger

Printed in USA

This book is dedicated to my son William Garrett Nichols and to all our sons and daughters. May they live by a code of ethics and honor that transcends the world of empty suits and the race to the unholy cubicle. May they dare to stare down oppression wherever it raises its loathsome face and may they be free to rebel, to ride, to live, and to love as true individuals.

CONTENTS

INTRODUCTION

IT IS A GOOD DAY TO DIE

NOW, MORE THAN EVER,
PEOPLE NEED A BACKBONE
AND A CODE TO LIVE BY.
THE ONE PERCENTER CODE
MAY WELL OFFER AN ANSWER,
SHOWING OUR YOUNG MEN
AND WOMEN THE WARRIOR'S
WAY IN A WORLD THAT HAS
LOST ITS EDGE.

A young warrior steps out of a crude hut to face the sunrise. Today is his day of days . . . today he will become a man. The rite of passage into manhood by various tribes has occurred in many lands and times. The common thread seems to be an experience of emotional and physical pain in which a boy passes a test of manhood to show courage.

The ancient Spartans believed that the only way to become a man was to become a soldier. Training began at age 7, when boys were taken from their families and placed in the agoge system. Spartan boys learned to be soldiers over the next 10 years. When a Spartan boy reached 18, he was sent into the wilderness with only a knife, and his goal was to kill as many helots (state-owned slaves) as possible without being detected.

The Maasai people of Kenya take boys between 10 and 15 years old to create a new warrior class. The night before the ceremony, the boys sleep outside in the forest. The next day, they drink a mixture of milk, cow's blood, and alcohol. Then the elders circumcise the boys before the entire tribe. If the boy flinches during the procedure, he is told that he will be disowned.

Among the Mandan Native American tribe living along the Missouri River in the Dakotas, a boy would fast for three days before the elders pierced his body with wooden splints. Ropes were extended from the roof of a hut and the boy was winched up into the air, hanging suspended by the splints. Despite the pain, the boy could not cry out. While hanging, more splints were hammered through his arms and legs, and the skulls of his grandfather and other ancestors were placed on the ends of the splints. Eventually, the young man fainted from loss of blood and pain, and the elders would pull him down. As if this were not enough, when he regained consciousness, the elders would chop off his pinky finger as a gift to the gods.

On a South Pacific island called Vanuatu, boys must jump head-first from a 100-foot wooden tower with vines tied to their ankles. The goal is to come as close to the ground as possible to show courage. The Satere-Mawe tribe of the Brazilian Amazon has a ritual whereby a boy must stick his hand in a glove woven with bullet ants and withstand their stings for more than 10 minutes without making a noise. The pain from these stings lasts more than 24 hours. All this makes a bar mitzvah seem like a fairly stress-free event.

When removed from the aboriginal peoples of this planet, man becomes a soft, flabby, weak creature. This is especially true in a privileged society like that found in the United States, where a metrosexual will squeal like a little bitch if the Vietnamese lady giving him his manicure cuts too close to his cuticle. Not only will such a pathetic creature be unable to stand even the mildest rite of passage, but if he even witnesses one, he will have to undergo years of therapy to cure his posttraumatic stress.

Modern men today have become weak, useless creatures. In large part that's because today's men have few rites of passage in our culture. Few groups of men supply the indoctrination into manhood that is required in these complex times. There is no sense of community or tribe for most boys on their way to adulthood, and, as such, the male (and female) population of our modern cities is sent into the world with no moral compass, adrift and lost.

I believe that rites of passage and a code of ethics and honor to live by are vital to human survival. I see our world going soft and offering no strength for present and future generations. I see today's kids spending too much time separated from elders who might teach them and peers they can relate to. I see too much of their young lives being spent in virtual worlds and online chat.

> Man becomes soft and weak in a privileged society like that found in the United States, where a metrosexual will squeal like a little bitch if his manicurist cuts too close to his cuticle.

Perhaps one answer to this problem is to look at a tribe that still exists in this land, one that offers a strong code of conduct based on respect, courage, and honor: namely the one percenter motorcycle club member. I believe that the biker lifestyle comprises many aspects of the warrior ethic from many lands and times, from the ancient Vikings, Huns, and Mongols, to the articles of pirates, the Code of Chivalry of knights, and even the famed Code of the West.

Now, more than ever, people need a backbone and a code to live by. *The One Percenter Code* may well offer an answer, showing our young men and women the warrior's way in a world that has lost its edge. May this be a guidebook based on truth and brotherhood for a world that is once again searching for its grail.

—Dave Nichols

1.
IN THE
BEGINNING

A LOOK AT THE RULES OF
SOCIETY, BOTH WRITTEN
AND UNWRITTEN, AND
WHERE THE CODE OF
THE BIKER FITS IN

> "A man's got to have a code,
> a creed to live by,
> no matter his job."
>
> —John Wayne

Why do we need rules in order to live together? Why do we follow rules? What is it about human beings that persuades us to adhere to a moral code? I mean, if you are a hermit and live alone in a cave somewhere in the wilderness without any human contact, I guess you can do as you please. But the minute any two human beings get within close proximity, the need for rules begins to crop up. This is apparent in creation myths the world over. Time and time again, we are shown that people, when left to their own devices, choose poorly and ruin their lives, the lives of their children, and the lives of those in their village or tribe, and even offend the gods.

Most mythic stories follow a simple "cause and effect" pattern; if you do something bad to someone, then the outcome is that something bad is likely to befall you. This is where we get such moral catchphrases as "Treat others as you would yourself" or "Do unto others as you would have them do unto you." This Golden Rule concept is the centerpiece of most religious practices and beliefs.

This should be simple enough for everyone to follow, but it doesn't always work as intended. The problem begins when various gods and goddesses grant mankind the ability to govern itself.

In most traditions we humans are given free will. Some religions actively encourage this; others accept it as a necessary evil, but at

> The minute any two human beings get within close proximity, the need for rules begins to crop up.

least they accept it. This is why many New Agers call Earth "a free-will planet." According to their worldview, we are among the few planets or dimensions in existence in which sentient life forms can literally create their own reality, moment by moment. Not that we're very good at doing so, at least judging by the consequences suffered by the characters in most mythic stories. Usually, according to the myths, our use of this God-given ability to create our own reality results in dire consequences. The end result of these myths seems to be that we humans are not quite ready to be god seeds.

The problem is not that we have free will to make our own choices; the problems come when we choose poorly. We take our free will and create hell rather than heaven on earth. Each of us, every day, decides if we are going to have a good and positive day, or one that is mired in depressing thoughts and actions. This has led to quarrels, bitterness, and, sometimes, revenge. We screw things up and that gives us drama, and drama, my friends, gives us stories.

THE PARABLE OF JAMES AND PAUL

A thousand years ago, if you lived in a community that was ruled by a king, you could go to that king to settle a quarrel. People were generally simple-minded farmers or shepherds, and they saw their king as an extension of divine intelligence. Based on this premise, I have devised the entirely contrived parable of Paul and James. Here's how it might have worked:

Paul shared grazing land with James, before the need for fences, and both men raised sheep. But every day, fewer and fewer of Paul's sheep seemed to be returning to the fold at his house. Then Paul noticed that James had a new ox cart and fine clothes for his wife. Paul got the idea that maybe James was selling some of his sheep. After all, before branding, one sheep looked very much like another sheep in a herd. When confronted, James told Paul he was full of hooey (an ancient phrase meaning mentally unbalanced). An argument ensued and Paul punched James in the eye.

Since their ability to render justice was extremely limited, the two men went into the village to seek the word of the king, for the word of the king was *law* in their valley. The king had a long list of people at court wishing to see him each day to settle similar societal quarrels and perceived injustices.

Paul and James waited in line for the better part of a day, shooting each other the occasional wicked glance. Paul was even considering buying a curse from the village wise woman to make James' teeth fall out if he didn't get satisfaction from the king. But he soon forgot such thoughts when a man and two women pleaded their case to the king. Apparently the man somehow had two wives and was giving neither any money. Before the invention of television, the king's court offered much entertainment.

When their time came to stand before his regal highness, the men bowed to show respect, and then, having heard it all in his tenure, the king asked the men their names. In order to be fair to both, the king asked James to tell his side of the story first, since James' name came before Paul's alphabetically and both men would see that this was a fair way to determine who should speak first.

"I am minding my own business," James began, "when my neighbor comes to me and accuses me of selling his sheep. He thinks I am more prosperous than he since I have a new ox cart and fine clothes for my wife. But the fact is, my wife's mother is very ill and, believing that she might die soon, gave me her ox cart and gave my wife some of her fine clothes."

The king then asked Paul to speak his piece. "I am noticing that many of my sheep are not coming home at night," Paul said as he pled his case. "My herd is getting smaller each day. I think my neighbor is selling my sheep. I have seen his mother-in-law, and though she is a grouchy old woman, she does not look sick to me."

Speaking out of turn, James yelled, "He poked my eye!"

When confronted, James told Paul he was full of hooey (an ancient phrase meaning mentally unbalanced). An argument ensued and Paul punched James in the eye.

Paul grabbed his neighbor by the neck and screamed, "He is full of hooey!" The assembled crowd in the court gasped appropriately.

Then the king gathered facts from both men and discovered that no fence or wall separates their land, that their sheep are not tagged for identification in any way, and that there is, in fact, no way to tell Paul's sheep apart from James' sheep. As a good and noble king and a fair judge, the king decided to make a trip out to the men's grazing land to see with his own eyes what was transpiring.

The next day, the king and his entourage followed Paul and James to their fields. The king saw that Paul's sheep do indeed seem to be wandering away over a hillside as if with a single-minded purpose. The king and his entourage followed the sheep over hill and valley for several hours. At last they reached the top of a hill and looked down into a glen that featured dense black-berry bushes. Here they witnessed many sheep happily eating the berries while others lay about sunning themselves with full bellies. "Here are your sheep," the king announced, defusing the situation. For accusing his neighbor and poking his eye, Paul must pay the king 10 of his sheep. The king also will allow James to smite Paul with a poke in the eye if he so chooses just to make sure that justice is done.

Now if this story of the two shepherds and the noble and just king sounds like a fairy tale told to children, it is. This is the sort of parable that parents have told their children for time out of mind to instill concepts of morality and proper behavior. This is why schools still insist our children read *Beowulf* or *The Legends of King Arthur and his Knights of the Round Table*. The roots of societal codes of conduct go back to our earliest tribes of people and to storytelling as a way to instill proper conduct. It is one of the ways that human beings develop character.

THE PARABLE OF MOOCH AND WEE WILLY

These parables still have something to offer us today. Take as an example an instance in which Mooch from the Devil's Wankers Motorcycle Club suspects his club brother Wee Willy of dipping into his stash of herbal relief. Wee Willy accuses Mooch of being full of hooey and Mooch pokes Wee Willy in the eye. Before events get out of hand and the clubhouse gets smashed in an epic brouhaha, cooler heads prevail; the brothers are subdued and the issue is brought before the chapter president at the next club meeting. In this case it turns out that Wee Willy really was pilfering Mooch's stash, and the club president orders Wee Willy to forfeit his private stash of the chronic to Mooch as reparation.

The more things change, it seems, the more they stay the same.

Assembling your custom chopper yourself was a way bikers earned street cred. It was a rite of passage in the One Percenter Code.

CODES OF CONDUCT

If you Google "Codes of Conduct," you will find lists of documents that endeavor to create and understand codes of conduct for schools and colleges, business corporations, military personnel, even U.S. judges. In its 2007 International Good Practice Guidance, "Defining and Developing an Effective Code of Conduct for Organizations," the International Federation of Accountants provided the following working definition:

Principles, values, standards, or rules of behavior that guide the decisions, procedures and systems of an organization in a way that (a) contributes to the welfare of its key stakeholders, and (b) respects the rights of all constituents affected by its operations.

"I ain't here for a long time, I'm here for a good time!" Biker truth at a Topanga Canyon party, circa 1977.

So where do these codes of ethical behavior come from? Is there a manual on how to be a good human? Many of our modern-day laws, beliefs, and rules go back to the Bible's Old and New Testaments, with their many parables and their famous Ten Commandments. These commandments point out the basic stuff, such as do not murder another human being, do not steal, do not commit adultery, do not covet anyone else's spouse or their stuff, that sort of thing. There's even a commandment that says to honor thy father and mother. You can bet somebody's mom snuck that one in.

Just to be clear, I'll paraphrase the original Ten Commandments listed in the Hebrew Bible:

1. Yahweh is number one. End of story.
2. Graven images are *verboten*.
3. No false swearing using the name of the Lord. Doesn't mention anything about true swearing, so that might be a gray area.
4. The Sabbath is for holy chilling out.
5. Honor thy father and mother.
6. No murdering anyone.
7. No adultery either.
8. No stealing.
9. No bearing false witness against your neighbor.
10. No coveting your neighbor's wife. Also, you're not supposed to covet his *ass* either, but back then *ass* had a very different meaning than today.

These same basic Ten Commandments are used not only in the Jewish faith, but also in the Christian faith, and though the commandments are a bit longer in the Quran, they serve the Muslim faith as well.

In addition to a lot of the same commandments in the Judeo-Christian traditions, the Ten Commandments of Buddhism add a few twists:

1. Do not become intoxicated.
2. Eat temperately and not at all in the afternoons.
3. Do not watch dancing, nor listen to singing or plays.

4. Wear no garlands, perfumes, or any adornments.
5. Sleep not in luxurious beds.
6. Accept no gold or silver.

Not sure I agree with the "Do not become intoxicated" bit, but for the most part these codes of conduct are fairly sensible.

Once God's various rules were etched in stone, as it were, mankind then set out to create its own rules of conduct and order, something lawmakers continue to create, control, and enforce to this very day. These various rules strive to define acceptable behavior and also point out unacceptable behavior. One such list of "no-nos" is the Seven Deadly Sins. These are, in no particular order, wrath, greed, sloth, pride, lust, envy, and gluttony. In other words, a lot of people's favorite things.

Things become even less fun when you go from the laws of God to the laws of man, many of which tend to be king-hell downers. Throughout history, people have taken their self-made laws and rules very seriously; these laws differ greatly from the casual guidelines of conduct handed down by God. Take traffic laws such as "Come to a complete stop at a stop sign," for example.

On pre-Evo Harleys, breakdowns were as common as oil leaks.

Another category of rules includes the Unwritten Rules, which cover everything from "Don't talk with your mouth full" to "Turn your cell phone off while in a movie theater."

CASTRATED SHEEP

In societies today, we have been programmed to accept that rules and laws are necessary evils that attempt to keep us from killing each other, robbing each other, and annoying each other by yapping on our cell phones in a movie theater. They are primarily invented to keep us safe. But this mollycoddling can go too far, castrating a society for its own good to give the illusion of safety. We have become a nation of sheep, happily giving up our freedoms in the name of something called "homeland security," which only offers the illusion of safety.

In reaction to the terrorist attacks of 9/11, President George W. Bush signed the U.S. Patriot Act into law on October 26, 2001. The title of the act is an acronym, which stands for "Uniting and Strengthening America by Providing Appropriate Tools Required to Intercept and Obstruct Terrorism."

Many of us felt that a better name would have been "Using Scary Assholes to Provoke A Totally Ridiculous, Idiotic, Oligarchy Takeover." The act dramatically increased the powers of law enforcement agencies, in the process radically diminishing our constitutional freedoms and rights.

I have a friend who lived through the German death camps during World War II. She has the numbers tattooed on her arm to prove it. When the Patriot Act was enacted, she told me, "This is how it started in Germany." *This is how it started* . . . those are some very scary words, and I believe her.

We have not just become a nation of sheep; we have become a nation of castrated sheep, and very few creatures like being castrated. Many people in our society chafe at the ever-increasing encroachment by the nanny state. When confronted with diminishing freedom, the rebel in us asks, "Where do the rules of the one percenter fit in?"

Following the attacks of 9/11, the one percenter found it increasingly hard to fit in. It wasn't just because they were anarchists, either. Even though he values freedom, the outlaw biker sees a need for rules. It's just that those rules follow an entirely different path than those of our homogenized society of twenty-first-century America. In this book we will talk about rules to be sure, but we are more interested in the underlying code of conduct that makes up biker morals. Where do the concepts that define that code come from and how did they become a part of biker culture? How is it that certain ideals have become bedrock in the outlaw world?

ANCIENT CODES

Much of the outlaw biker code comes from long ago, gleaned from ancient tribes that shared some of the same rebel tendencies. These were people who would not go quietly into the night, but raged with the dazzling fire of nonconformity and lived outside the box, sometimes way outside the box when compared to civilized society.

> We have become a nation of sheep, happily giving up our freedoms in the name of something called "homeland security," which only offers the illusion of safety.

For every breakdown there's always a great story
and few laughs to be had . . . usually after
the fact.

It is no coincidence that many one percenter clubs take their names from such original wild ones as the Vikings, knights, and pagan gods. Likewise, it is no surprise that the One Percenter Code contains elements of earlier codes, such as the knight's Code of Chivalry, a moral system that went beyond mere rules of combat and included qualities that have become synonymous with knighthood, such as bravery, courtesy, honor, and gallantry toward women.

You can also find elements of the pirate's code in the One Percenter Code. During the Golden Age of Piracy (1640 to 1730), pirates operated under a set of rules called the Charter Party, Custom of the Coast, or Jamaica Discipline. These codes of conduct eventually became known as the articles, or the pirate's code. The articles varied from captain to captain, but all versions include how treasure would be shared, compensation for injuries during a voyage, and discipline aboard ship.

The One Percenter Code embodies elements of more recent codes too. In our quest to find the One Percenter Code, we will note many similarities in the legendary Code of the West. This was a system of morality based on the primacy of the individual, one in which a man's word was his bond, insisting that men stand for what is right and protect the weak and the innocent. We'll find that today's free-thinkers and rebels on wheels have much in common with the beliefs of the American cowboys.

Chronicled by western writer Zane Grey in his 1934 novel *The Code of the West*, no written code ever actually existed as a rule-book for right action. However, the pioneers who lived in the West were bound by these unwritten rules that centered on hospitality, fair play, loyalty, respect for the land, and observation of the Golden Rule. Many of the rules in the Code of the West were distilled from common sense—or horse sense—including such universal truths as "look out for your own," "don't be ungrateful," and "your word is your bond." (More on the Code of the West in Chapter Four).

Today we tell stories and offer morality plays through motion pictures. Ask any biker to name his favorite films, and westerns will be at the top of his list. For me, the Italian westerns directed by Sergio Leone are personal favorites, including *Fistful of Dollars*, *For a Few Dollars More*, and *The Good, the Bad, and the Ugly*. There's something about Clint Eastwood that really strikes a chord with bikers. Maybe it's that Clint always plays rebellious loners, from the man with no name and Dirty Harry to Walt Kowalski in *Gran Torino*.

Speaking about the philosophical allure of portraying loners in westerns, Eastwood has said, "Westerns. A period gone by, the pio-neer, the loner operating by himself, without benefit of society. It usually has something to do with some sort of vengeance; he takes care of the vengeance himself, doesn't call the police. Like Robin Hood. It's the last masculine frontier. Romantic myth." Substitute

In our quest to find the One Percenter Code, we will note many similarities in the legendary Code of the West.

bikers, and you'll see why the Code of the West is so prominent in the biker code.

OUTLAW MOTORCYCLE CLUB RULES, REGULATIONS, AND BYLAWS

In *The One Percenter Code* we will concentrate on the evolution of the biker way of life, we will separate outlaw club rules from the overarching biker code of conduct, and uncover rules of the road, a code aimed at keeping you alive while riding on two wheels. We'll also look at the separate reality found in the American prison system

One percenters have nobility that is reminiscent of knights on iron steeds.

and discover that the biker code has made its way into that closed and dangerous society.

As mentioned in my book, *One Percenter: The Legend of the Outlaw Biker*, every one percenter motorcycle club has rules and regulations. Though one percenters are antiestablishment rebels who go their own way, every organization has rules, and the motorcycle club is no exception. In fact, the bylaws of the average motorcycle club are reminiscent of the articles mentioned earlier that a sailor had to sign before becoming part of the crew on a pirate ship.

What follows is a composite listing of some club rules taken from many different American one percenter clubs. They have been edited in order to be generic and would fit most clubs, but they certainly do not cover all the rules of all motorcycle clubs. During church night (the night of the club's official meeting), the officers of the club hold sway in much the same way as they would in any civic organization, such as the Eagles, Jaycees, or Moose Lodge. Robert's Rules of Order apply. The president of the club, along with a vice president, secretary, sergeant-at-arms, and treasurer, move the meeting along. Cookies are not served afterward.

- The rules of the club are strictly enforced. Anyone breaking them will be dealt with by a committee made up of original members. The breaking of club rules could result in dismissal or suspension.
- Failure to pay club dues may result in dismissal.
- All members will wear the club's colors in the prescribed manner, with the club logo, club name, and chapter displayed as shown in the club articles.
- Prospects will be allowed to wear only the club bottom rocker and a prospect patch.
- If a group or individual citizen (nonclub member) attacks any member, the entire club shall stand behind him and fight if necessary. However, if the member is drunk and aggressive and purposely starts an argument, the rest of the club will remove him or step between him and the aggressor before trouble starts.
- No member will disgrace the club by being a coward. This goes for prospects as well.
- No member will destroy club property purposely.
- Members are expected to help out their brothers, no matter what.

The T-shirt reads: "I'd rather see my sister in a whorehouse than my brother on a Jap bike." Hate to be this guy's sister.

Though one percenters are anti-establishment rebels who go their own way, every organization has rules, and the motorcycle club is no exception.

- No member will go against anything the club has voted for and passed.
- No members will get together on their own and plan something for themselves on club rides. Their idea will be brought up for the whole club and the club will participate in anything decided upon.
- The club will always stay together on rides, runs, and events and will not fraternize with rival clubs. Members may only leave the group if allowed to by the president or whoever is in charge. All club members will leave together. Anyone staying behind will do so at his own risk and can expect no help. (Sort of like the pirate's code of "He who falls behind, is left behind.")
- Members are expected to attend mandatory rides and church night meetings. You must have a good reason for not attending, such as work, sickness, bike not running, or jail.
- Failure of paying dues within two weeks of them being due will result in suspension. If dues are not paid within two months, the member will be out of the club. The only exception is when a member is in jail, in which case no dues are expected, or if a member is out of town, in which case dues will be expected upon his return.
- No female will be a member of the club. Wives and girlfriends will be allowed at certain club runs and parties, as decided by the officers of the club. In some cases, wives and girlfriends may be allowed to wear support shirts, "property of" patches, and tattoos.
- Anyone wishing to become a member of the club must prospect for a period of no less than six months and as long as the officers of the club deem appropriate. When voting a prospect in, the vote of members will be taken as an opinion. The officers of the club have final say as to whether a prospect is voted into the club or not.
- Prospects are expected to participate in club affairs, rides, meetings, etc. They must have a running motorcycle (some clubs insist the bike be of American origin, which means Indian, Harley-Davidson, or Victory, while others might allow foreign bikes only if they were built by World War II allies, which pretty much means Triumph, Norton, or Ural. Virtually no clubs allow Japanese, German, or Italian motorcycles) and

There's nothing in the world like riding down the highway in a pack of loud Harleys.

show a sincere interest in the club and bikes. Prospects will stand behind the club and its members and will go along with what the majority of the club decides (much like the democracy found on pirate ships).

- If the club calls a ride, all members will attend unless excused by an officer of the club. If a member's bike is down, he may pack on another member's bike or ride in the chase truck (usually loaded with girlfriends, tools, and beer).
- On weekend rides, members should be able to take time off of work to attend. If this is impossible and more than four members cannot attend the run, the club will wait for them the following day.
- Church meetings will be closed to all except members, prospects, and those who have business with the club.
- Any nonmembers attending club bike runs are expected to follow club rules. If another club is attending a club ride and breaks the club's riding rules, the club will stop and let them continue by themselves.
- Talking during meetings will be kept to a minimum. The sergeant-at-arms will evict anyone who disrupts a meeting.
- No one will pass the road captain on a club ride.

- The entire membership will vote on where the club will go on club rides.
- The treasurer will keep a clear record of all money paid in and out and will report on the balance at club meetings.
- All members will attend church meetings on their motorcycles, weather permitting.
- A member whose motorcycle is down for an extended period of time may be suspended until his bike is in working order.
- No one will lend his colors to anyone who is not a member of the club.
- No one will bring heat to the house (meaning that no member will cause trouble or deal in illegal activities that might draw police to the club).
- Members will wear their club colors on club rides.
- Anyone leaving town for more than six months is expected to leave his colors with the president until his return.
- Any member missing a meeting for any reason will be fined unless he is in the hospital, in jail, or out of town for a period of time.
- No prospect or member is allowed to use heroin in any form. Hypes will be immediately kicked out of the club.
- No explosives will be thrown into campfires for any reason (some clubs state that the fine for such activity is an ass-whipping).
- Guns that are carried on runs will not be displayed after 6 p.m.
- Club members will not fight each other using weapons. Fights with members are to be one on one, and prospects are regarded the same as members.
- If a club member fights a member of a different chapter of the same club, a fine will be taken from each man by the treasurer of his club and he may be suspended for a time determined by officers of the club.
- No narcotic burns. When making deals, people get what they are promised or the deal is off. Breaking this law will get you kicked out of most clubs.
- All fines will be paid to the club treasurer within 30 days. Monies will be held to use for upcoming runs.
- If you are kicked out of the club, you will remain out for one year before being accepted back into the same chapter. Club tattoos will reflect in and out dates when the member quits.

- If a member is permanently kicked out of the club (*out bad), the club tattoo will be completely covered, or an X will be tattooed through the club tattoo at discretion of the chapter.

THE CODE OF THE MODERN WARRIOR

As you can see, simple rules are enforced for the sake of sanity, even in a one percenter motorcycle club. Now let's move away from written rules of rebels past and begin to delve into what we might call a code for the modern warrior. After all, that's why you're reading this book, isn't it? I suspect that you are reading these words because you have a yearning for a code of conduct that defines and transcends that of mainstream society. Perhaps, as seen in this chapter, the One Percenter Code may borrow from some of history's—the codes of chivalry, articles of piracy, and certainly from the Code of the West. You may well feel that there is something missing in our modern code of ethics and that our children need guidelines to live by that instill the best of what has come before in diverse rites of passage, indoctrination, and simple, truthful ways of being.

You may, in fact, feel lost in this age of everything-going-faster-and-faster for no apparent reason. That's understandable. This society in which we live offers little to sustain us and yet asks everything of us. We work so that we may pay taxes for wars we don't believe in. We pay health insurance so that doctors can leech extra money from us when they discover we have life-threatening illnesses. We work so that the machine of government can coerce us and tell us what to do. We work so that everything we don't believe in can live and prosper while we struggle. So the first thing I'm going to tell you is this: Life doesn't have to be this way.

I suspect that you, like me, might not fit in very well with the average text-messaging metrosexual who just accidentally dropped

---

* There are basically two ways to get out of a one percenter motorcycle club. If you leave honorably, it is most likely that you have served the club well for many years and are still considered a brother, though you have retired. The other way is to be "out bad." This means you have been kicked out of the club for some reason. At best, to be out bad means that you are shunned by the club as an outcast.

> This society in which
> we live offers little
> to sustain us and yet
> asks everything of us.

his Bluetooth into his mocha latte. That you might feel that there is a general lack of discipline in today's soft cubicle occupant, which a true code of conduct might provide. That what is often lacking in video game–playing teens is a real sense of character. That there is much more to life than the race to the cubicle so that you can afford to buy stuff you really don't need. That the mindless drone of television has bred a generation of lazy couch potatoes with no moral center, or as a one percenter might say, "People who aren't about anything."

Perhaps you are sick and tired of being treated as a terrorist every time you try to get on an airplane, removing your shoes and belts and lifting your arms in supplication as you are x-rayed and body scanned. When we are led about by the nose like brain-dead cattle in a so-called free society, giving up our freedoms with mindless abandon, it makes us realize that the terrorists have won. They took away our freedom and that is exactly what they wanted to do.

I'm not saying that America is no longer a free country, but I see that the erosion of our freedoms comes as a result of a lack of the very spirit that created this country. Do you think Daniel Boone would lay down his rifle and hatchet to get on a stagecoach that might be stopped at any moment by highwaymen? No. How would he protect and defend his fellow travelers with merely a cell phone and an iPod?

In short, perhaps you are looking for a place to stand, broadsword drawn against all comers, in a time that has no use for you. You are looking for a few like-minded individuals who have your back no matter what. You don't want to quietly let go of the warrior within you. You have a rebel yell that needs to be heard. You often wonder why you were born into a time and place like this because, try though you might, you just don't fit in with the rest of the sheep. You are a wolf, my brother.

Welcome, friend. You don't have to grind down your fangs and remove your claws. There is a way to live in the world as an outlaw, outside the confines of polite society, to live proudly and even prosper with your middle finger still raised high.

I ask that you forget everything you know, or think you know, about the iconic bad boy image of the outlaw biker. As we peel away the layers of this amazing tribe, you will find brotherhood, honesty, great faith, and loyalty beyond measure.

It is time to take the journey. We're going to find the One Percenter Code together on perilous seas and across the wild west. No one is going to ask you to lay down your weapons or your rights here.

While a Wide Glide might not be anyone's first choice for trail riding, any biker worth his or her salt knows how to handle his or her machine when the pavement ends.

2.
RITES OF PASSAGE

THE REASONS WHY
ONE PERCENTERS CHOOSE
TO LIVE IN THE MARGINS OF
SOCIETY AND THE THINGS THAT
HAPPEN THAT MAKE THEM
ABANDON THE LIFE OF
AN ORDINARY CITIZEN

We begin our quest on the very day you are reading this. The time is now and the place is anywhere you might be living on planet Earth. No matter if you live in a tiny village or a thriving metropolis, somewhere near you there are people living in abject poverty. Some are homeless, many will go to bed hungry, most have lost hope, and all are seeking a way out of their situation.

There are many people alive today in your town, in your city, in your state, in your country, and in your world who are seeking connection, seeking an extended family, praying to whatever god they know, seeking to belong to something. That is why so many young people today are searching for something to belong to and why many of them join street gangs.

Inner-city kids, especially minorities, are the most at risk to join gangs since many of their fathers either split or are in jail. Today, more than 1.5 million people are cooling their heels in American prisons and 44 percent of them are black. Our cities have become war zones for kids from broken homes. The kids are fodder for gangs; they stand no chance of surviving on the streets if they don't have a gang to back them up.

The gang acts as a surrogate family, offering support for kids with low self-esteem. Why do so many kids today have low self-esteem?

> Our cities have become war zones for kids from broken homes. The kids are fodder for gangs; they stand no chance of surviving on the streets if they don't have a gang to back them up.

Mainly because of the system they grow up in. In this country, the education system is tightly regimented with a bias toward math and science. If you are a creative person, or good with your hands, or a farmer, you don't fit into the curriculum and you are an outcast. Many special classes, such as shop classes and art and music classes, have been eliminated in our schools because of budgets cut to the bone. So if you happen to have a talent as a mechanic or artist of any kind, you're pretty much out of luck; there is no respect for your talent. You have no value to the system. Chances are, like a lot of kids, you will fall between the cracks because the system is flawed.

THE RULE OF COMMUNITY

What do kids do when there is nothing to feed their souls, when the system places no value on what they have to offer? There is nothing for them to strive for that means anything. Today, our society and our government are trying to replace spirit with consumerism, and if you don't fit into the cookie cutter, you are cast out of society. Street gangs are waiting for kids who don't fit into the cookie cutter, offering them a sense of family and community, albeit a twisted one.

Do you know the rule of community? It has existed in many tribes and in many lands. It has been followed by the Viking berserkers of old as well as pirates, soldiers, street gangs, police officers, church groups, and bikers. Especially bikers. This rule of community is the rule of family—no matter what group you are a part of, you "take care of your own." The rule of community is the primary rule of the one percenter.

Though the world may be against him, every biker knows that his club has his back. The sense of brotherhood and family found in a motorcycle club has a powerful attraction. But in order to understand why this rule is important and a cornerstone of the One Percenter Code, we must first understand basic human needs. I'm not talking about wants; I'm talking about basic needs that we all share. Like Mick Jagger sang, "You can't always get what you want. But if you try sometimes, you just might find, you get what you need."

There is a psychological theory based on Abraham Maslow's paper, "A Theory of Human Motivation," published in 1943, that is commonly called Maslow's hierarchy of needs. Maslow is known as the leader of the humanist school of psychology and was a leader in the human potential movement.

His theory describes the various stages of human growth and is often represented by a pyramid. The base of the pyramid represents the most fundamental needs, such as our need for air to breathe, water, food, and shelter. People who are just barely getting by are at the base of the pyramid. When you are at this level, you are only

"Stop in the name of the law!" Yeah, fat chance, pal; we're on our way to a helmet protest run.

Hangin' with brothers and friends, tellin' tales
about the Panhead that got away.

concerned with your own survival. You can't worry about higher
pursuits, such as creativity and art, or following a spiritual path
when you don't know where your next meal is coming from. In fact,
if you are at the base level of Maslow's pyramid, you're too busy
trying to stay alive to do anything else.

Maslow suggested that these most basic of human needs must
first be met before a person can move upward on the pyramid. He
also noticed that some people have a stronger drive to go beyond
the scope of basic needs in order to strive for something better. He
called this *metamotivation*. So at the bottom of Maslow's pyramid

> The rule of community is the rule of family—no matter what group you are a part of, you "take care of your own." The rule of community is the primary rule of the one percenter.

you have physiological needs, the literal requirements for human survival, without which the body cannot function.

Once a person's physical needs are met, they move up to safety needs. These have to do with our need for our environment to be predictable and orderly. We want to wake up in the same bed, with a roof over our heads, not starving and freezing to death in some alley. In your profession you want to have some sort of job security, health insurance, and maybe a retirement plan. So this part of the pyramid has to do with personal security, financial security, health, and well-being.

Once our basic survival and security needs are met, we move up to a social level. Here we can afford to breathe easy enough to look for some sense of belonging. This is hardwired into our brains, not only because there is safety in numbers, but because the human animal has existed in tribes since there have been bipedal hairless apes walking around on this planet. Maslow's hierarchy on this level includes friendship and its balm for loneliness. It includes intimacy, sharing, and, ultimately, family.

At the core of every human is the need to belong and to be accepted by our peers. We all want to be a part of something, whether it's at the office, at church, on sports teams, in clubs, or, especially, in families. So, Maslow tells us, once we have air to breathe, water to drink, food to eat, clothes to wear (so we're safe from the elements), a place to sleep with a roof over our heads, and some way to make a living, we feel safe enough to open up to others, and the first thing we strive for is connection. We all want to belong.

> At the core of every human is the need to belong and to be accepted by our peers.

Without acceptance from others, we become lonely and depressed. The need not to be lonely is so powerful that people will sometimes put a sense of belonging over their need for security, meaning that the need for community can be promoted from a higher-level need to a basic need. Because this need is so primal, it's only natural that we devote much energy to seeking out like-minded individuals and groups in which we can belong.

NEVER GO AGAINST THE FAMILY

One percenters will tell you that their club brothers are their family, that they would take a bullet for any one of them. What inspires such loyalty? It is similar to the bond that's formed when men and women serve together in the armed forces and have been in harm's way. The bond is formed out of hard-earned respect for the other. It is that absolute knowing that your brother has your back no matter what happens. It is a safety net like no other.

I can't tell you how many times I have seen this fierce loyalty put to the test. I've seen bikers walk into a hornet's nest and fight their way out, tooth and nail. I've seen a lone biker get pushed too far in an outmatched fight and then his brothers jump in without knowing who started the ruckus or why it happened. You see, in the biker world, it doesn't matter who started it; we know who will finish it. I've even seen a dude who was completely in the wrong start an incident that should never have happened, the kind of thing that puts the club in a bad light. While that one percenter's brothers will have a talk with him about his actions later, at the moment when the blood is up, all members wade into the fray regardless of who is right

Every motorcycle club has an enforcer or two to make sure that everyone behaves.

or wrong: "All for one and one for all!" One percenters are loyal to the core. Remember these three words: loyalty, honor, and respect. We'll talk much about them in this book.

If you ask a biker to describe a true brother, he will tell you that a true brother is someone you can call at three in the morning and wake up out of a dead sleep to tell him he needs to get over to your house pronto and to bring a gun . . . and he'll be there, no questions asked. Lock and load, baby.

There are five levels to Maslow's hierarchy of needs pyramid, and so far, we have visited three of them. The fourth level is concerned

Rob Roloff of the Modified Motorcycle Association of California on the courthouse steps, fighting for bikers' freedoms.

with esteem. This is where the one percenter's world really kicks in because it is here that we seek to be respected and gain self-esteem and self-respect. We need to be accepted and valued by others, and in order to have that need met, we enter into activities that give us a sense of contribution so we feel valued by those who are important to us.

RESPECT

Today, many young people have low self-esteem and a feeling of being inferior to others. This can cause all kinds of problems. One percenters don't have this problem because the hierarchy in a motor-cycle club teaches each man to stand his ground, to stand for something, to be about something, and to hold his mud. People who have low self-esteem are looking for respect from others; one percenters know without a doubt that they have the respect of their brothers. In fact, you cannot become a fully patched member of an outlaw motorcycle club without the full acceptance of everyone in the club. They are committed to you and you to them.

What do I mean when I say that a man has to stand for something and be about something? A great example may be found in the 1995 film *Braveheart*, when Mel Gibson's character William Wallace gives a memorable speech to brace his men for battle:

> Wallace: *I see a whole army of my countrymen here in defiance of tyranny. You have come to fight as free men, and free men you are. What would you do without freedom? Will you fight?*
>
> Veteran soldier: *Fight? Against that? No, we will run; and we will live.*
>
> Wallace: *Aye, fight and you may die. Run and you'll live—least a while. And dying in your beds many years from now, would you be willing to trade all the days from this day to that for one chance, just one chance, to come back here and tell our enemies that they may take our lives, but they'll never take our freedom!*

Ah, freedom, that elusive, vaporous thing. Yet who among us would not lay down his life in defense of it? How many thousands have done just that? How many have laid down their own personal needs and wants for a grander cause? How many have given up their "self" for such an ideal as freedom? This is where a human being becomes something greater than the self and steps into his true power and potential.

> You cannot become a fully patched member of an outlaw motorcycle club without the full acceptance of everyone in the club. They are committed to you and you to them.

Many people who suffer from low self-esteem are always trying to prove themselves to the world. They seek fame and fortune. They are never comfortable in their own skin, never happy with what they have. They may achieve the fame and fortunes they seek, but they'll always have a big empty hole in their hearts until they accept themselves. It's like the Hollywood starlet who will never think she's pretty enough, even though she's on the cover of every movie magazine in the country, because she's insecure.

Inner confidence—a healthy need for self-respect, strength, mastery, independence, and freedom—is the opposite of the need for esteem based on validation from others. Such inner confidence is achieved through personal experience. The one percenter is that rarest of breed that exists both within a group of like-minded individuals with strict codes of conduct, but is also his own man. I think that is the prime reason that many men in society today fear bikers. They are the sheep looking at the wolf, knowing they will never be one. It's hard to imagine what it would be like to be free, "when you are bought and sold in the marketplace," as Jack Nicholson says in

The slogan of bikers' rights groups is "Let those who ride decide"—though it never hurts to keep a skid lid handy for the hardbellies.

> The one percenter is that rarest of breed that exists both within a group of like-minded individuals with strict codes of conduct, but is also his own man.

the 1969 film *Easy Rider*. "But when they see a free individual . . . it's gonna scare 'em."

Finally, the top tier of Maslow's pyramid is the need for self-actualization. It is here that we step into our full potential to become who we really are. We strip away much of society's restrictive suit of conformity. Though we must still live in the world, we don't need to be of the world.

It is here that, having risen through the lower levels and mastering them, we find the freedom to express ourselves through creating art, poetry, and music. This is the realm of invention and imagination. It is also where we attain the realization that we are made of god stuff, that we are not separate from the creator.

The levels of Maslow's pyramid are in many ways similar to the chakra system mentioned in Hindu practices. The word *chakra* derives from the Sanskrit word for *wheel* or *turning* and refers to the "force centers" that are believed to exist in the etheric body. This aural body is the first layer of the energy field that surrounds your body like an invisible cocoon.

Just as the base of Maslow's pyramid focuses on survival mode, so the base or "root" chakra is related to survival. Just as the next step up the pyramid involves safety and security, the second chakra at the sacrum involves base emotional needs, and so on. Perhaps it is not a coincidence that Maslow's pyramid features evolutionary levels that move from humanity's most base to most enlightened in much the same way that the chakra system does. Perhaps he was trying to bring these spiritual concepts to mainstream academia without the lens of religious practice or belief.

TAKING CHARGE

The One Percenter Code is a system of conduct and belief that states that each man is the captain of his destiny. Because bikers stand up for their own, and also stand tall and proud as individuals, they have tapped into their entelechy. Aristotle defined *entelechy* as a thing that has reached a condition of being fully realized, the optimal template of its being. In other words, creatures that have reached a state of enetelechy exhibit themselves as larger than life, mythic beings. Bikers are as mythic in character as the marauding

Maslow should have added smoking, drinking, and riding motorcycles to his hierarchy of needs.

> The one percenter does not
> buy into systematic conformity
> that tells us "Don't do this
> and don't do that."

Vikings, or the Knights of the Round Table, or the pirates of the Spanish Main, or cowboys on the open plains. By developing a separate reality that exists alongside that of the soulless masses, bikers create their own reality.

Many people who become bikers do so because they don't fit in with the masses. Bikers are by nature a rebellious breed, and each of us who follows the beat of a different drummer, in this case the steady beat of a Harley-Davidson V-twin engine, will tell you that we decided not to buy into the illusions that we were being handed by society, governments, and religions. We question authority and we question reality on a daily basis.

The illusions that are forced on us by society, governments, and religions are the basis for a great deal of human suffering on this planet. The one percenter does not buy into systematic conformity that tells us "Don't do this and don't do that." Naturally, the forces that benefit from this system have set up what I call the Fox News/ CNN Reality, which is media-enforced dogma designed to get us to conform like good puppies while keeping us from realizing our true potential. As long as they can get you to buy into the fake consumer-driven reality they preach, you can be controlled and further manipulated.

DROWNING IN SHIT

As Americans, most of us walk the straight-and-narrow path, not because we genuinely want to be good people, but because we are afraid of what will happen if we don't. Most Americans don't fear

She's either having the time of her life or trying not to shit her pants. Maybe both.

prison as much as they fear losing their job and thereby losing their stuff. Yes, our stuff—all that ridiculous bric-a-brac that we find on eBay, our gas-guzzling cars, our laptops, and our cell phones.

Annie Leonard's amazing short film, *The Story of Stuff*, explains how our consumer society began and why we are all so obsessed with being good consumers, buying and hoarding stuff. Annie discovered that our consumer-driven society is in trouble. Basically, our planet has a finite amount of stuff to begin with and we have a linear system on a finite planet and we want it to run forever. It can't.

Of the 100 largest economies on earth, 51 are corporations, which make them bigger than the world's governments. These corporations are only interested in profits, so they have to keeping selling stuff to us. The problem is that we're running out of resources. This film illustrates that we are cutting and mining and hauling and trashing the place so fast that we're undermining the planet's very ability to sustain life.

Care for a few bits of trivia? You can dole these facts out at your next cocktail party: Only 4 percent of our original forests are left in the United States. The United States has 5 percent of the world's population, but we're consuming 30 percent of the earth's resources. If everyone alive today on earth consumed at our rate, we would need three to five planets in order to produce the necessary resources. But wait, there's more. More than 75 percent of global fisheries are at or beyond capacity. An amazing 80 percent of the world's forests are gone, and in the Amazon, we're losing 2,000 trees a minute.

Once we extract the materials to produce our stuff, an interesting thing happens. According to Annie, "We use energy to mix toxic chemicals in with the natural resources to make toxic contaminated products." There are more than 100,000 synthetic chemicals in commerce today and we don't know what impact these chemicals will have on our health or environment. Certain chemicals, such as brominated flame retardants (BFR), are in our computers, appliances, couches, mattresses, even in some of our pillows. And guess what? BFRs are neurotoxins, as in toxic to our brains!

Toxins of all kinds build up in our food and concentrate in our bodies. In fact, because all of our stuff and food is filled with toxic material, the highest level of toxic contaminants has been found in human breast milk. And of course, the people who get saturated with the most toxic chemicals are factory workers, many of whom are women of reproductive age.

> The reality that most Americans live in is an illusion or several illusions.

Once all the consumer goods end up at stores for us to buy and bring home, a whopping 99 percent are thrown away within six months. The average American consumes twice as much as they did 50 years ago. How did this happen?

"Shortly after World War II, these guys were figuring out how to ramp up the U.S. economy," Annie tells us.

Retailing analyst Victor Lebow was quoted as saying, "Our enormously productive economy demands that we make consumption our way of life, that we convert the buying and use of goods into rituals, that we seek our spiritual satisfaction, our ego satisfaction, in consumption. We need things consumed, burned up, replaced, and discarded at an ever-accelerating rate."

President Dwight D. Eisenhower's Council of Economic Advisors chairman said, "The American economy's ultimate purpose is to produce more consumer goods." Thus the great minds of U.S. government turned us away from spiritual pursuits in favor of buying a never-ending supply of stuff based on planned obsolescence and perceived obsolescence. Why else would fashions change every three months and computers and cell phones need to be upgraded every year?

Americans clearly need to create a *new* American Dream that is not based on buying more stuff, but rather living more fulfilling lives with an enhanced sense of community that offers real connection for our hearts and spirits. One way to make this happen is to make it cool to be sustainable as a species. Not long ago, Americans thought it was cool to own gas-guzzling SUVs because they saw all the rap artists and sports players driving them. Now, with gasoline hovering at five bucks a gallon, it's suddenly cool to drive a Prius and the SUVs are dinosaurs.

Soon you will be hearing a lot about green chemistry, zero waste, renewable energy, and the like. What would be really cool is if we could figure this out before we trash our planet so completely that our species becomes extinct.

Many Americans continue to identify who they are with what they drive and what they wear. Take away their stuff and you've got nothing—an empty suit. But the reality that most Americans live in is an illusion or several illusions.

REALITY: WHAT A CONCEPT

In his *Conversations with God* book series, author Neale Donald Walsch talks at length about the illusions that we live with in society today. He calls these "the ten illusions of humans," and they are important to note here since I believe that many of these man-made "grand illusions" are keys to the One Percenter Code. I'm not saying that most bikers have put their feeling of rebellion against the system into such eloquent words as Mr. Walsch's, or even that they are specifically aware that they create their own rebel reality, but they live these principles nonetheless.

According to Walsch, the first human illusion is the illusion of need. He believes that the concept of need is an illusion, that we have everything we require within ourselves. Of course, Maslow would point out that our bodies do need nourishment and we do need shelter from the elements or we will die, but Walsch's point is still worth considering because conning us into thinking that we need things we really don't need is how the system enslaves us. Naturally, the system wants us to believe that there is need because without the illusion of need, we wouldn't buy all that stuff and the consumer-driven machine of society would crumble.

Walsch's second illusion is that failure exists. If need does not exist, how can failure exist? Failure is a human concept based on a set of rules or principles that do not relate to the one percenter. According to Walsch, there are experiences in life that we call failures based on judgments we have made created out of misunderstandings.

If we rethink failure as just a learning experience, then the concept of failure is an illusion. If the system cannot convince us that we have failed somehow, how can it keep its boot on our backs?

> Failure is a human concept based on a set of rules or principles that do not relate to the one percenter.

With more and more of us becoming bald-headed gray beards, it's getting increasingly rare to see a biker with a mane like this.

The third illusion is that separation exists. If you imagine that you are a mere human animal with needs, wants, and tragic failures, then you imagine that you are separate from God. Because Walsch believes that God is all that is, God wants for nothing and cannot fail. So, we fall into the illusion that we are "other than God." We are lowly, we are not worthy, we come from dust and to dust return. This, of course, makes us easier to control.

It is also incorrect. The concept that we are separate from everything, that we are separate from our friends, our neighbors, our community, our country, and our universe, is, according to Walsch (and Arthur Schopenhaur before him, and Immanuel Kant before him, and Plato before him), a crock of shit.

The fourth illusion is that insufficiency exists. The illusion of insufficiency tells us that we had better stockpile some karma because there will never be enough no matter what. We are insufficient to our spouses, to our kids, and to God. Guess what? It's a lie.

But it motivates us to supersize that McFatAss meal we're shoveling into our pie hole.

The fifth illusion is that requirement exists. Here we find the concept that if there is something we lack, we can acquire it by doing or becoming something. If we buy into the illusion that there is not enough stuff, then we think perhaps that there is stuff we can acquire in order to have enough stuff. Again, Walsch thinks this is pure, unadulterated bullshit. We don't have to own a flat-screen TV to be cool; we don't have to drive Jaguars to show the world we have made it. But if we let the powers that be trick us into thinking we really do need to acquire more stuff, it makes it a lot easier for the world's corporations to sell us stuff.

The sixth illusion is that judgment exists. Human beings have built an entire universe around the concept of judgment. The Bible tells us that God is vengeful and wrathful. Don't piss him off or he shall smite thee! The God of the Old Testament judges you, and if he finds you guilty of not living up to his rules and expectations, well, ask not for whom his cosmic shithammer tolls because it tolls for thee. This idea is based on the concept that you will be kept out of heaven unless you "earn" your place there.

Therefore, you have to meet the requirements, and those change from religion to religion, whether that means abstaining from eating meat on Friday during Lent, eating pork pretty much any

> Maybe there is some god or gods (depending on your particular belief system) up in heaven somewhere deciding who is going to win the football game on Sunday and who is going to get hit by a bus.

time, or forgetting to whip out your prayer rug and bend down toward Mecca at some set time each day. So which is it? Most likely you'll think it is whichever version you were taught as a youngster, and all those other versions are nonsense. This brings to mind Joseph Campbell's definition of mythology: other people's religion. But if you step outside of your own biases and look at the situation logically, you'll see that it's highly unlikely that any one religious system is more or less "true" than any others. Since they often contradict each other, they can't all be true, right? Well, chew on this a moment: Perhaps none of them are true, at least as far as we understand the word *true*. There is good reason to believe that many of these rules came about for political or economic reasons. Take, for example, the idea of not eating meat on Friday during Lent. The official Catholic explanation for this is because Christ died on a Friday, we should abstain from shedding blood on Friday, but research indicates that the real reason for this is that fish merchants convinced the church to ban the eating of meat in order to increase the sales of their products.

When you start to peel the onion of religious rules and regulations, you find many, many instances where there was an earthly reason behind what was supposedly a divine order. It happens often enough to make me question all those rules and regulations. Like the stuff in Leviticus about burning a stool if a menstruating woman sits on it—seems like a waste of a perfectly good stool to me. I could be wrong; perhaps I will burn in hell for not fasting during Ramadan, but I doubt it. I'll take my chances and not worry about being judged by anybody else's interpretation of God.

The seventh illusion is condemnation. If there is a judgment system, there also must be a system of rewards and punishments. Maybe there is some god (or gods, depending on your particular belief system) up in heaven somewhere deciding who is going to win the football game on Sunday and who is going to get hit by a bus. But again, if you look at the situation without the filter of your preconceived notions, you can see a pragmatic reason to make people believe this is true. If you have a population that believes every edict issued by a religious organization, that's pretty damned handy for controlling said population. You use the promise of heaven for the carrot and the threat of hell for the stick. If, for example, I could

> Having ridden with death
> on his shoulders each time
> he throws a leg over a
> motorcycle, he lives life to
> the fullest because this is
> all there is . . . breathe,
> life, freedom!

convince you that if you didn't buy 100 copies of this book during Lent you would burn in hell, but if you did buy the books you would be guaranteed a place in the kingdom of heaven, that would be a profitable trick on my part.

The trickle-down theory is in place with this illusion. For instance, if God can reward and punish you, if God can uplift or condemn, so can I. This allows me to look down on others because the rules say my neighbor is not good enough. This illusion has created a very judgmental society.

The eighth illusion is that conditionality exists. This follows judgment and condemnation and is built upon those illusions. The idea here is that the universe is built on the barter system. "I will give you love, *if* you will do the following . . ." But in no major religion does God love you *if*. The Christian Bible teaches that God's love is unconditional.

The ninth illusion is that superiority exists. This one is absolutely ridiculous since a thing cannot be superior to itself, and as the above points out, all things are one.

The one percenter has been downtrodden, put down, beat down, and disrespected. He has been jailed, called a lowlife scum, and threatened in every way imaginable. Because of this, the one percenter looks down on no one because he's been there. The one percenter is not on this planet to judge or condemn anyone because he has been judged and condemned. Having ridden with death on his shoulders each time he throws a leg over a motorcycle, he lives life to the fullest because this is all there is . . . breathe, life, freedom!

The tenth illusion is that ignorance exists. This is the illusion that supposes that you do not know that all the rest of this is an illusion. It supposes that you cannot know the truth because you are ignorant of the truth of what *is* and how the universe works. If this book were a movie, this would be the part where the phone would ring, you would answer, and a voice would say, "What if I were to tell you that the reality you think you know is just an illusion and that the real world is happening all around you while you sleep?" Creepy. Sounds a lot like *The Matrix*, doesn't it? And yet, that is exactly the reality that most of the empty suits out there are living. The one percenter took that phone call long ago.

THE RIGHT STUFF

I bring all this up because I believe that the one percenter essentially creates the world in which he wishes to live, designing a reality that is free of Walsch's ten illusions. The one percenter's view of reality is markedly different from the reality enforced by the media. Bikers remind me of cowboys in that they are a natural part of the landscape. They exist, as did the Native Americans, with respect for nature in an existence that is not based in greed.

The truth is that we are all made of God stuff. The atoms and molecules that make up your body are the same stuff that stars are made out of. It is impossible for you to be separate from creation. It is impossible that you are separate from all that is. Somehow bikers know this. There is something about riding down a ribbon of highway on a motorcycle that frees your soul. You have time to think, to take in the sights, sounds, and smells that are all around you every second. You commune with the road and with your machine. Soon, the separation between yourself and nature blurs and you lose the *self* and become part of the *all*.

One percenters think outside the box of regimented society and dare to be that most dreaded of all outlaws, the freethinker. Society has never known what to do with us because we don't play by the rules. We run with scissors. School principals just shake their heads at us, but we are easy to understand when you think of bikers as wild animals in a cage. Ever see a video of wild wolves running free

> One percenters don't like
> to stay in the box and once
> we have come out of the box,
> there is no way in hell you
> can ever fit us back into it.

in the woods? Ever see a video of wolves trapped in a cage? A cage is what society represents to us, so it's no wonder that one percenters break out and run free.

I don't think that rebels necessarily choose to live in the margins of society, abandoning the life of an ordinary citizen as much as the fact that there is never any choice. One percenters don't like to stay in the box and once we have come out of the box, there is no way in hell you can ever fit us back into it.

Like wolves, we run free.

3.
THE CODE IS THE LAW

IN MANY WAYS THE CODE OF THE OUTLAW BIKER IS EVEN STRICTER AND MORE RIGIDLY ENFORCED THAN THE RULES OF ORDINARY SOCIETY.

> "The only rules that really matter are these . . . what a man can do and what a man can't do."
>
> —Captain Jack Sparrow

've said it before: One percenters are wolves in a land of sheep. While wolves make the sheep nervous, they also create balance in the world and even offer an insight that would not exist otherwise. The one percenter represents that small percentage of people who will not conform.

The term "one percenter" first came about as the result of what has been called the Hollister riot. Many believe that the incident in Hollister singlehandedly created an unwholesome image for both Harley-Davidson and motorcyclists in general. There's no doubt that the image of the leather-clad hellion blasting down the road on a loud customized Harley as he thundered across the landscape on his way to rape America's daughters was invented by the media due to some mildly antisocial activities that took place at an AMA Gypsy Tour on July 4, 1947, in Hollister, California. Much has been written about this incident, though little that the media of the day reported regarding the Hollister Riot was actually true.

The city fathers in Hollister had put on motorcycle races long before the alleged riot and never had any problems with rowdy riders. As the short version of the story goes, World War II servicemen and flyers returned from the war changed men. They were ready to raise a little hell and some of them had a passion for the white-knuckle thrills that could be found by riding big chopped Harley-Davidsons (known then and now as Hogs).

These guys would strip everything they could off of Harley dressers to make the bikes lighter. Off went the windshields, saddlebags, and front fenders. They would cut off, or "bob," the back fender and these custom "bobbers" became the forerunners to the choppers of the 1960s and '70s.

These AMA-dubbed "outlaws" were guys from motorcycle clubs like the Boozefighters, Galloping Gooses, Jackrabbits, and the 13 Rebels. Out of the nearly 3,000 riders who came to watch the races and be part of the rally, the outlaw riders only amounted to a handful. The misdemeanors that supposedly took place over the course of the weekend were pretty much of the public intoxication or drunk and disorderly variety. For example, the police cited one guy for trying to urinate into the radiator of his truck. There was racing in the streets, whooping, hollering, and plenty of drinking, but not anything more outrageous than you'd see at a college frat party. About the worst thing that happened was that somebody stole a cop's hat. According to original Boozefighter Gil Armas, someone opened the front door to Johnny's Bar on the main street and said, "Come on in!" Gil rode his bike right up the curb, into the bar, and propped it up against the bar to order a drink (an act that would later be immortalized in the Stanley Kramer film *The Wild One*).

One percenters span the globe. Here we see an Angels' camp in South Copenhagen.

> Gil rode his bike right up the curb, into the bar, and propped it up against the bar to order a drink (an act that would later be immortalized in the Stanley Kramer film *The Wild One*).

THE STEREOTYPE FROM HELL

So how did this weekend of innocent shenanigans transform into a riot and turn these fun-loving patriots on wheels into demon bikers from hell? Ahh, you have the media to thank for that. *San Francisco Chronicle* photographer Barney Peterson was at the rally looking for a story but needed a catchy image to get his editor's attention. He got an idea and pushed a bunch of empty beer bottles over to a Harley that was parked at the curb. He then carefully choreographed the scene to create the effect of a drunken orgy, enlisting the help of a rather large inebriated fellow named Eddie Davenport who just happened to be strolling down the sidewalk. Peterson had Davenport pose on the bike, which wasn't even his.

The picture and sensationalized story that blew the events at the rally out of proportion appeared in the July 1947 issue of *Life* magazine, and the die was cast. Almost overnight, motorcyclists became crazed blood-thirsty bikers to the public at large. Lock your doors, guard your daughters, and run for your life because outlaw bikers on loud, nasty motorcycles were coming to raid your town!

To combat this new surly image, the AMA issued a now famous press release explaining that the "rough" element of motorcycling public amounted to only 1 percent of the total riding community. The organization insinuated that most motorcyclists were good, clean, God-fearing Americans with jobs and families. They didn't modify their motorcycles, take the Lord's name in vain, or fornicate outside the sanctity of holy matrimony.

"Keep yer mitts off a my ol' lady!" In all times and in all lands, ladies love outlaws.

Naturally, the "outlaw clubs" that were sprouting up across the country liked the idea of being the 1 percent that your momma warned you about and the term "one percenter" was born. Being a one percenter became a proud badge of honor to all those bikers who felt disenfranchised by society. The loners and outsiders finally had a name and standard with which they could identify.

So the term "one percenter" is synonymous with the 1 percent of humanity that doesn't play by the rules: the rebels, the outlaws, the freethinkers, all those disenchanted with society's rat race game. Since 1947, those who have dared to live outside of the conventions of polite society have had a handle to hang their hat on.

> Once we bought into the concept that all that matters is working hard to buy stuff we don't need in order to keep up with an impossible ideal of being the rich Americans we see on TV sitcoms and in movies, we will do anything to keep our stuff.

Today, a one percenter is anyone who still has the fire of rebellion burning in his belly. So let's define our terms here. What is the One Percenter Code, really? It is a way of life taught through the school of hard knocks, learned on the streets with a graduate degree in tough luck and dogged determination. It goes part and parcel with the American Dream of our fathers; we as individuals, as a people, and as a nation can do anything if we set our minds to it. And one of the things all one percenters have in common is that we don't want to play by the Man's rules.

Unfortunately, once the plans were laid to base the postwar American Dream on consumerism rather than spirit, it only took one generation for us to lose our spunk and become a nation of sheep. You see, once we bought into the concept that all that matters is working hard to buy stuff we don't need in order to keep up with an impossible ideal of being the rich Americans we see on TV sitcoms and in movies, we will do anything to keep our stuff. We'll even give up our freedoms. Just please don't take our stuff . . .

So what does that leave us with? We have become a nation addicted to fast food and gasoline, striving for a whiter smile while our freedoms are taken away day by day. Most Americans would never dream of fighting the system they helped put in power, because if they did, they'd be thrown in jail, lose their jobs, lose their friends, lose their spouses, but most importantly, they'd lose their stuff.

One percenters don't give a shit about stuff. The code is the law, and one percenters live and die by the code.

TRUE COLORS

You've heard the phrase "showing their true colors," right? In a one percenter motorcycle club, members wear their true colors on their backs for all to see. These patches are more than the club banner; they are the summation of a way of life, rich in life and proud in death.

As mentioned earlier, the core of the One Percenter Code is that you take care of your own. All else revolves around that concept. I remember a brother who went to jail for a little while, unfortunately leaving his wife and two little girls to fend for themselves. He knew the club had his back. Club members made sure his family got groceries every week, that the wife and kids were looked after and cared for. He got visits while in jail, money, smokes, whatever he needed. And it's not just the club members who pitch in to help; all the members' families get involved as well. Members' ol' ladies babysat the little girls, took them to movies and for pizza while the mom worked. When that bro got out of jail, he knew without a doubt that he was loved by his club. The one percenter club provides modern-day proof of the idea that it takes a village to raise a child, and when it comes to the children of one percenters, those kids are raised with a code of ethics that will serve them all their lives.

Every one percenter knows that it is his job to school the young on what it means to live by the code. At school, the children of one percenters are taught not to start fights, but if a fight happens, to show no quarter. That earns respect with the kids at school, and that respect in turn ensures that children from one percenter families aren't picked on. The same thing happens in prison. People take

> Every one percenter knows that it is his job to school the young on what it means to live by the code.

No brother left behind. The paint on this gas
tank is from a David Mann painting that shows the
old-school way to tow a busted scoot.

kindness for weakness and will fuck with you if they think you are
weak. The unhappy truth is that if people can take advantage of
you, they will. But one percenters are wolves, remember? A sheep
that dares to cross a wolf will find itself as lunch for the pack.

If you are the member of a one percenter motorcycle club, that
club is your family and you would lay down your life for any of your
brothers. What are the rules of any family? There are certain things
that are true at the core of any family group. I asked a number of
one percenter motorcycle club members from a wide range of clubs
all across the country to give me one rule they would want to pass

Ridin' like a bat out of hell on a righteous
Shovelhead. It doesn't get any better than this!

on. I chose a cross section of bikers, from prospects to presidents. You'll find that these rules run the gamut from club business to rules within society, including the biker philosophy of life and death. Here's what true one percenters had to say about honor and honesty, and living the One Percenter Code:

- Take care of your own and take care of each other because in this big weird world, it's nice to have a family you can count on.
- Family business stays inside the family. You don't tell outsiders about your family, how much money you make, or where the bodies are buried.
- Protect your family at all costs. There is nothing you wouldn't do for your family. Always have your brother's back. When your brother is in need, you are expected to help him.
- Even when one of your brothers is wrong, you stand by him. You can ask questions later.
- Never lie to your family. Never cheat or steal from a brother or the club.
- Take care of business. If you aren't up to what it takes to ride with us, go join the Harley Owners Group.

- Once a club rule is made, never go against that rule.
- When going anywhere with the club, stay together. There is strength in numbers.
- When a meeting of the club is called, you are expected to be there and to participate. If you don't want to give the club your whole heart, you don't need to be in the club.
- Never bring heat to the house. Ever!
- Defend yourself and your club brothers, no questions asked.
- Never steal a motorcycle. Bike thieves are worse than horse thieves.
- Take a man based on who he is today, not on who he was in the past (which also goes with the next rule . . .).
- Don't ask a man a lot of questions about himself.
- Don't make a threat unless you can back it up.
- When coming up behind a biker, make yourself known. In other words, no surprises.
- Never "eye fuck" a one percenter. (Act respectful and sincere around bikers. Don't challenge them with your eyes . . . or anything else for that matter. It will just end up getting you thumped.)
- Don't run off at the mouth. You can always tell a prospect who will not be making the grade to fully patched member. It's the guy who talks too much.
- Be glad for what you have in life. It can all be taken away from you in a heartbeat. This is true both because the Man can take everything away from you in an instant and because bikers know that death rides with them around every corner. All it takes is a little loose gravel in a turn to meet your maker.
- Always be courageous. Cowards are not tolerated in any one percenter club.
- Always stop and help those in need. I can't tell you how many times club brothers stop along the highway to help people who are stranded in their cars. But you never hear about that in the news, do ya? It's like the old saying goes, "When we do good, no one remembers. When we do bad, no one forgets."
- Always be grateful. There will always be people who are better off than you are and folks who are not as well off. When you need a hand up, remember there are those who need you to reach down to give them a hand up as well.

> As usually happens, every rule means that someone somewhere did something stupid so that such a rule was needed in the first place.

- Always be pleasant and respectful to people (outsiders) when wearing the club patch. You are representing the club and want to show everyone that we are knights of the road, not the gangsters they fear.
- Never sit on another man's motorcycle without permission. You'll find yourself on the ground bleeding real fast.
- Be there for a brother when he needs you, no questions asked. When a brother calls for your help, you go. Period.
- Loyalty above all else. Be loyal to the bone to your club, your brothers, and those you ride with.
- The Golden Rule applies to all bikers: Do unto others as you would have them do unto you. When in doubt, knock 'em out!
- Your word is all you have. Your word is your bond.

Those are all good rules and there are plenty of reasons for them. You can bet that most of them came about out of sheer need. As usually happens, every rule means that someone somewhere did something stupid so that such a rule was needed in the first place.

HANG TOGETHER OR HANG ALONE

As I mentioned in Chapter One, kids today join street gangs because they are looking for family and community. They want to belong to something. They are seeking connection. They also need protection. The same is true of one percenter motorcycle clubs. Ask any biker to tell you stories of how they have been discriminated against because they ride motorcycles and you will be opening the floodgates, a deluge of stories about being beat up by rednecks, shot at by street gangs, or, especially, constantly harassed by the police.

The fact is that when you are a lone biker on the road, if things go south you might just end up dead in a ditch somewhere. This was especially true in the 1960s and '70s. However, if you are with a group of bikers, there is indeed safety in numbers.

Ask any biker who rides a chopped Harley about police harassment. You'll get variations of the same story. Every time you go out for a ride, some cop pulls you over to do a field search, checking you for drugs and weapons, running a check on you for warrants and violations. Your bike will be inspected for broken head- or taillights, loud pipes, seats that are too low, or apehanger handlebars that are too high.

Before Harley-Davidson came out with the Evolution motor in the 1980s and every doctor and lawyer in the country ran out and bought a Softail, it was common for a lone biker out on the road to be stopped several times during a single afternoon ride. A lot of bikers joined motorcycle clubs in the 1970s not only to ride with a righteous club, but for the protection it offered them.

RICO

Interestingly, riding with a club was like going from the frying pan into the fire, thanks to something known as the RICO Act. In 1970, Congress passed the Racketeer Influenced and Corrupt Organizations (RICO) Act, Title 18, United States Code, Sections 1961–1968. The idea was to curtail organized crime, which was impacting the American economy, and the goal was to basically eliminate the Mafia and other organized crime racketeers.

Under the RICO Act, a person or group who commits any 2 of 35 crimes—27 federal crimes and 8 state crimes—within a 10-year period and, in the opinion of the U.S. attorney bringing the case, has committed those crimes with similar purpose or results can be charged with racketeering. Those found guilty of racketeering can be fined up to $25,000 and/or sentenced to 20 years in prison. In addition, the racketeer must forfeit all ill-gotten gains and interest in any business gained through a pattern of "racketeering activity."

The act also contains a civil component that allows plaintiffs to sue for triple damages.

When the U.S. attorney decides to indict someone under RICO, he has the option of seeking a pretrial restraining order or injunction to prevent the transfer of potentially forfeitable property, as well as requiring the defendant to put up a performance bond. This provision is intended to force a defendant to plead guilty before indictment.

What is racketeering? It is defined as any act or threat involving gambling, murder, kidnapping, arson, robbery, bribery, extortion, dealing in obscene material, or dealing in a controlled substance.

One of the most successful applications of RICO has been when it is used to indict or sanction individuals for their behavior and actions committed against witnesses and victims in alleged retaliation or retribution for cooperating with law enforcement or intelligence agencies.

When the court perceives a "pattern of racketeering," it can use the RICO Act to run surveillance on any group that it believes might be guilty of participating in organized crime. Use of the RICO Act has put away crime bosses to be sure, but it has also been used to target motorcycle clubs and street gangs. Any member of a one percenter motorcycle club can be convicted of conspiracy and can be thought to be guilty by association with known felons in their organization. Not long after RICO was enacted, there were a lot of motorcycle club brothers in penitentiaries across this country. This made many club members on the outside go into hiding. The American government had effectively put its thumb on one percenter motorcycle clubs across the country.

Another big problem that has surfaced in recent years is that a number of high-profile one percenter clubs have been infiltrated by police officers and special agents pretending to be bikers in order to prospect for a club, and they have even become fully patched members. The undercover agents have then spent months, even years, gathering information on these clubs in order to prove that they are involved in racketeering. The informant often turns club members against the club so that all sorts of snitches and rats abound.

Invariably, two interesting things come out of these infiltrations of clubs; one is that most of the charges against club members ultimately have to be dropped for lack of solid evidence, and the other is that these informants end up writing books hoping to cash in on selling people out. What a country.

The more infamous of these books include the following:

• *Angels of Death: Inside the Biker Gang's Crime Empire* by Julian Sher and William Marsden. This book takes readers inside the Arizona chapter of the Hells Angels and the biggest American police undercover operation to infiltrate the club.

Go ahead, ask these guys if they're gay. I dare ya.

Because of the constant hassle from law-enforcement officials, bikers have become very tightlipped about the motorcycle lifestyle, what they do, and how they live.

- *Running with the Devil: The True Story of the ATF's Infiltration of the Hells Angels* by Kerrie Droban. More on the infiltration of the Arizona chapter by several cops who designed a fake Mexican motorcycle club in order to hang with the Angels. This led to a major bust in 2003 in which ATF agents arrested 50 people.
- *Under and Alone* by William Queen. ATF agent William Queen infiltrates the San Fernando chapter of the Mongols MC. He lives as a one percenter, gets inside, becomes a member, and gets confused because he has to bust men that have truly become his brothers. What a piece o' shit!
- *A Wayward Angel* by George Wethern. This book is billed as a brutal inside account of the Hells Angels as told by one of the club's most notorious leaders.
- *No Angel: My Harrowing Undercover Journey to the Inner Circle of the Hells Angel* by Jay Dobyns. Here's another would-be author trying to make a buck by telling you how he became a righteous club brother, then ratted everybody out. Blech!

MAD DOGS AND BIKERS

Because of the constant hassle from law-enforcement officials, bikers have become very tightlipped about the motorcycle lifestyle, what they do, and how they live. It is no wonder that one percenter clubs are strict about rules and enforce them diligently. You will also find that though they are hunted like mad dogs and hated by normal citizens, there is no more dedicated group on earth than bikers when it comes to doing good for a good cause.

Bikers have always been givers when it comes to charities, especially if the charities have to do with children. For the last six years I've had the honor of sponsoring the Seattle Children's Ride, which supports the Seattle Children's Hospital. Monies raised by this annual motorcycle run go toward making sure that no child is ever turned away for treatment. The ride brings in nearly half a million dollars a year and is the second largest fundraiser the hospital has. Not bad for a bunch of no-good bikers, eh?

Bikers of every kind and creed join together each year to give back and to do something good in the world, and because of charity rides and events around the country, the media has begun to see a positive side to all of us wild ones. While there are literally hundreds of motorcycle groups and organizations currently producing motorcycle charity events from coast to coast, the following are four of my favorites.

1. The Love Ride
   Benefiting Autism Speaks
   Started by Glendale Harley's Oliver Shokouh 25 years ago, this ride has brought in more than $22 million.
   Held in Glendale, California, in November
   www.glendaleharley.com

2. Toys in the Sun Run
   Benefiting the Joe Dimaggio Children's Hospital Foundation
   This run has been going on for 24 years and brings in more than $400,000.
   Held in Sunrise, Florida, in December
   www.toysinthesunrun.com

3. Rip's B.A.D. (Bikers Against Diabetes) Ride
   Benefiting juvenile diabetes
   Started by *Easyriders* magazine's Rip Rose, this event has brought in hundreds of thousands of dollars in the past 14 years.
   Held in Irvine, California, in June
   http://badride.diabetes.org

4. Children's Ride
   Benefiting Seattle Children's Hospital
   The Imagine Guild has been holding this three-day party for 15 years. It brings in more than half a million dollars each year for unsupported care for kids with life-threatening diseases.
   Held in Seattle, Washington, in June
   www.childrens-ride.com

In this chapter we have learned that one percenters are, as a whole, very much like the ideal of the cowboy of old, with many of the same codes of conduct. While you would not want to disrespect a one percenter, you can also see that they stand up for their own, that they are loyal to a fault, and that they are loving and giving to children and those in need. You can also see that they are not to be trifled with. Unlike the average Joe Citizen out there, one percenters are not afraid of the kind of lawsuits that happen when someone disrespects them and they end up having to thump somebody a little bit. While the fear of lawyers and courts keep most citizens in line, the one percenter doesn't give a rat's ass about such things.

There is nothing you wouldn't do for your biker family. Always have your brother's back.

> Generally, one percenters
> will treat everyone fairly
> unless a person proves himself
> to be a weak piece of shit, in
> which case they are happy to
> run the guy off.

The important thing to remember here is that one percenters don't give a fuck for authority and authority figures. However, bikers don't go out of their way to cause trouble either. Generally, one percenters will treat everyone fairly unless a person proves himself to be a weak piece of shit, in which case they are happy to run the guy off. The rule here is "don't step over the line." The late gonzo journalist Hunter S. Thompson got properly and famously thumped by a club when he stepped out of line. It didn't matter if he was famous, or a writer; it didn't matter if he had a lawyer or friends in high places. He stepped over the line and paid the price of a sound beating.

As a general rule, bikers hate uppity, superior people who automatically assume they are better than others. Even though the media has created the bad boy image of the American biker and many bikers do nothing to discourage this stereotype, we are insulted when being stereotyped, just as anyone would be.

BEING ABOUT SOMETHING

What does "being about something" really mean? Among bikers and many others who live outside of the all-American norm, there is the point of view suggesting that in order to fit into society, you have to check your brain at the door and just become a good, compliant consumer, a.k.a. "sheep." Don't ask questions, don't make waves, just do as you are told. Good citizens follow rules mindlessly and use the sidewalks and crosswalks. When faced with a sign that says, "Please stay off the grass," you'll find a one percenter taking a piss on it. We can't help it. We have a problem with being told what to do.

One percenters see the rule-following masses as empty suits, walking in a straight line, not making waves and certainly not making a difference. We see them walking right off a cliff, following other empty suit lemmings, happily throwing themselves into oblivion. The problem is that we see them taking us all with them.

We see straight society consuming everything, like a cancer, using up all of the planet's resources, filling their McMansions with glittery stuff they don't need in order to fill a giant hole in their hearts that they have no idea how to deal with. In other words, they aren't about anything. They are not doing one thing that will make this world a better place for their children and all others to whom they leave the wreckage they've created.

When asked, many one percenters will tell you they believe in the reality set practiced by some Native Americans. Bikers are much more at home and at peace with the idea that we are part of the land and have a respect for it. Just as the Native Americans do, one percenters don't take or use what they don't need. If we kill a deer for food, you can bet we'll use every piece of the animal, from the antlers and hide to all the meat. When Native American tribes hunted and killed an animal for their village, they thanked the spirit of the animal for all it would provide, knowing that we are all one family and all share the same planet. The empty suits don't understand this. They think their burgers come from the great god McDonalds.

In other words, bikers see the majority of those living by the rules, those empty suits, as not being about anything at all. They are

> Looking at the beliefs of Native Americans is one of the best ways to understand the heart of the One Percenter Code.

taking up space, they are devouring all our world's resources, they are using up the air . . . but they might as well be dead. Adversely, one percenters see their belief system as being about something, standing for something, being individuals who live by a code of honor and conduct. The One Percenter Code offers a holistic point of view. We want the planet to be here for our children and their children.

Looking at the beliefs of Native Americans is one of the best ways to understand the heart of the One Percenter Code. Of course, there are as many Native American beliefs as there are Native American tribes, and the hundreds of belief systems that evolved among the indigenous people of North America have a wide variety of traditions, but, at the risk of overgeneralizing, most have some variations of the following ideas.

Most Native American belief systems teach that everything is sacred, from the smallest plant and animal to the tallest mountain and the sky, and that there is a lesson to be learned in every experience. Everything has a purpose. This leads to codes of conduct very much like those followed by the one percenter, a code based on honor, love, and respect for all living things.

As such, most bikers and most Native Americans are in touch with every living thing, knowing that we are a part of everything and that everything is a part of us. Didn't know that bikers were such spiritual cats, did you?

We also respect our elders, those who keep our culture alive and hold the answers. The late Navajo/Apache medicine man White Feather has been quoted as saying, "Native American isn't blood; it is what is in the heart. The love for the land, the respect for it, those who inhabit it, and the respect and acknowledgement of the spirits and the elders. That is what it is to be Indian." The same may be said for the one percenter.

In Chapter One I mentioned the Ten Commandments that are the basis for Judeo-Christian ethical law and belief. Most Native American cultures also have sets of commandments given to them by the creator at the time of creation. These include the following:

- Treat the Earth and all that dwell thereon with respect.
- Remain close to the Great Spirit.
- Show great respect for your fellow beings.

If you'd even think about screwing with a brother's bike, you'd deserve the brutal ass-pounding that you'd get.

- Work together for the benefit of all mankind.
- Give assistance and kindness wherever needed.
- Do what you know to be right.
- Look after the well-being of mind and body.
- Dedicate a share of your efforts to the greater good.
- Be truthful and honest at all times.
- Take full responsibility for your actions.

Just as this Native American list of commandments is very close to the ideals of the One Percenter Code, there is also a Native American code of ethics. Obviously this differs from group to group, but most such codes contain a variation of ideals that are, in many ways, synonymous with the spiritual code of the one percenter. This list of ethics usually includes some form of the following rules:

- Give thanks each day for the life you have and for all life, for the good things the creator has given you, and for the opportunity to grow each day.
- Consider your thoughts and actions of the past day and seek the courage and strength to be a better person.

- Seek the things that will benefit everyone.
- Show honor and respect for other people, other life, and all things. Showing respect is a basic law of life. Special respect should be given to elders and parents.
- Touch nothing that belongs to someone else without permission, or an understanding between you.
- Respect the privacy of every person; never intrude on a person's quiet moment or personal space.
- Never walk between or interrupt people who are conversing.
- Speak with reverence in the presence of elders, strangers, or others to whom special respect is due.
- Do not speak unless invited to do so at gatherings where elders are present (a good rule for prospects).
- Never speak about others in a negative way, whether they are present or not.
- Treat the Earth and all of her aspects as your mother. Show deep respect for the mineral world, the plant world, and the animal world. Do nothing to pollute our Mother. Rise up with wisdom to defend her.
- Show deep respect for the beliefs and religion of others.
- Listen with courtesy to what others say, even if you feel that what they are saying is worthless. Listen with your heart.
- Respect the wisdom of the people in council (or on church night).
- Once you give an idea to a council meeting, it no longer belongs to you. It belongs to the people.
- Respect demands that you listen intently to the ideas of others in council and that you do not insist that your idea prevail. Indeed you should freely support the ideas of others if they are true and good, even if those ideas are different from the ones you have contributed.
- Be truthful at all times and under all conditions.
- The hurt of one is the hurt of all; the honor of one is the honor of all.
- Receive strangers and outsiders with a loving heart and as members of the human family.
- All the races and tribes in the world are like the different colored flowers of one meadow. All are beautiful. As children of the creator they must all be respected.

> When we as a country care for each other with the same passion and dedication found in a one percenter motorcycle club, we will take the first step in caring for our community and our world.

- To serve others, to be of some use to family, community, nation, and the world, is one of the main purposes for which human beings have been created. Do not fill yourself with your own affairs and forget your most important talks. True happiness comes only to those who dedicate their lives to the service of others.
- Observe moderation and balance in all things.
- Know those things that lead to your well-being and those things that lead to your destruction.
- Listen to and follow the guidance given to your heart. Expect guidance to come in many forms—in prayer, in dreams, in times of quiet solitude, and in the words and deeds of wise elders and friends.

If only humankind would follow these simple rules, our interactions with each other and the world would be much more peaceful and respectful. It always amazes me that in our fast-paced society of never-ending connection through smart phones and iPads and laptops and "friending" on Facebook, how little true connection we have with one another.

I live in a relatively small town of about 20,000 in southern Oregon, and I am truly impressed with how many things there are to do as a community here. No matter what your interests are, there are groups to join and ways to be a part of the community. People here are encouraged to get away from the "virtual world" on the Internet and interact with their neighbors. We have potluck dinners in the city park, we have block parties, we have a free "green show" of live entertainment every evening at 6 p.m. during summer months. There is a plethora of community theater shows, art walks, and parades for the Fourth of July, Halloween, and Christmas. Local bikers have rides from our Harley dealership nearly every weekend and many of those rides are charity events for a good cause.

My point is that we all need to get out there and connect with each other more. No matter where you live or what you're into, becoming part of something you believe in is very much a part of the One Percenter Code. No man is an island and no biker has to be a lone wolf, howling in the wilderness.

Since America became a consumer society after World War II, focused on buying happiness, our people became takers rather than caregivers of the land and all our animal brothers and sisters. We take, use up, and throw away rather than give back. If we are to survive as a nation, we would do well to learn a few lessons from our Native American brothers and take a few hints from the One Percenter Code. When we as a country care for each other with the same passion and dedication found in a one percenter motorcycle club, we will take the first step in caring for our community and our world.

Things a cage driver takes for granted, like being able to drink while driving, require a certain degree of resourcefulness on a Harley.

4.
THE CODE OF
THE WEST

ONE PERCENTER
MOTORCYCLE CLUBS
FIRST CAME TO PROMINENCE
IN CALIFORNIA. WHILE THIS
WAS IN PART BECAUSE THE
MILD CLIMATE ENCOURAGED
MOTORCYCLE RIDING, IT ALSO
REFLECTS THE OUTLAW SPIRIT
OF THE AMERICAN WEST.

Every day is a perfect day to ride in southern California. During those long winter months when most of the country is covered in snow and northern bikers are taking their scooters apart for a rebuild, riders in southern California can ride 365 days a year. Even the coldest day during a Malibu winter is still a glorious day to be on a motorcycle compared to the same December day in Minnesota. Because bikers in California can ride many more months of each year than can riders in northern states, it's easy to see why Kustom Kulture grew up in southern California, also known as SoCal.

Kustom Kulture (with the double "k") is that rich mix of spicy and irreverent art by the likes of Robert Williams and The Pizz and wild custom cars and bikes by Ed Roth, Von Dutch, Dean Jeffries, and their ilk. The subculture is a hodgepodge of rockabilly music and greasers, wild tattoos, and mindblowing art that has seen a real resurgence in recent years. It was—and is—a very California-based invention.

BOOZEFIGHTERS

When motorhead veterans of World War II came home to California, they started fooling around with customizing cars and motorcycles to make them go faster and look cooler, and the hot rod and chopper scene sprouted up practically overnight. California has always been the hotbed of the custom scene. Once a new custom trend catches on in SoCal, it slowly makes its way eastward. Eventually, the trends that are cool out west end up mutating as they travel east and wind up in New York. But the hottest trends usually start in southern California first.

In the mid-1940s, returning servicemen who fought for freedom during the war were looking for a taste of freedom of their own and many found that riding an American V-twin motorcycle offered both thrills and a sense of freedom. Because these vets had been through the horrors of war, they discovered that they had a hard time relating to the average citizen, so they tended to hang out together. Many veterans felt like outsiders and sought the solace of being with like-minded brothers; their passion for motorcycles and the comradeship they felt for each other provided seed for the creation of motorcycle clubs.

Interestingly, after every war that American soldiers have fought since World War II, there has always been a percentage of soldiers who come home and start riding motorcycles. It's as if only the white-knuckle thrills of riding big Harleys can calm their inner wolf. Naturally, many motorcycle clubs have grown up around such groups of vets.

> After every war that American soldiers have fought since World War II, there has always been a percentage of soldiers who come home and start riding motorcycles.

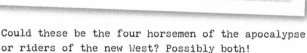

Could these be the four horsemen of the apocalypse or riders of the new West? Possibly both!

Early SoCal motorcycle clubs included the 13 Rebels, the Yellow Jackets, and Orange County Motorcycle Club, which all existed long before the Boozefighters of Hollister fame appeared. Other early SoCal clubs included the Rams, Checkers, North Hollywood Crotch Cannibals, and the Galloping Gooses. In 1949, just two years after the Boozefighters made the scene, a close-knit group of bikers out in San Bernardino started up the Hells Angels (more on that later).

As I mentioned in Chapter Three, the summer of 1946 marks the true birth of the one percenter, since that was when the Boozefighters MC came into being, leading up to the Hollister riot in 1947. As the story goes, a group of war veterans and their friends were sitting in the All-American Bar in South Central Los Angeles. The place was an old gas station with a bar attached in back. Most of the guys hanging out had two things in common: They had been through the war and they loved to race around on motorcycles. The "Big A," as patrons called the place, was a destination for bikers, and if you weren't a vet or into bikes you had no business being there.

Some of these guys had been riding motorcycles together since 1939, calling themselves The Characters. Wino Willie Forkner, J. D. Cameron and his brother Jim, Jack Lilly, and a few others were having several beers and were trying to come up with a name for their group of riders. Willie had been thrown out of another motor-cycle club for getting drunk and sneaking into an AMA-sanctioned race, causing a scene.

A very drunk fellow named Walt Porter was sitting with his head on the bar, half-listening to all the talk about names for a new bike club. He is said to have raised up his head and uttered, "You might as well call yourselves the Boozefighters, 'cause all you ever do is sit around the bar and fight that booze." The name stuck and the Boozefighters were born. Certainly many motorcycle clubs had come before, but the original Boozefighters and those clubs that came after them marked a change in the evolution of motorcycling because they became associated with the terms "outlaw biker" and "one percenter."

The term "outlaw" really referred to the fact that outlaw bikers were those who did not race at AMA-sanctioned field meets. They were racers outside the convention of the AMA's rules and regulations and therefore the bad boys, that 1 percent of motorcyclists who caused all the trouble.

The cowboy way tells us to live each day with courage, assist others in need, and always finish what you start.

CHOPPING AND BOBBING

Motorcycle clubs were at the forefront of creating the look of bobbers and choppers that is so popular today. Customizing really began as a way to make motorcycles faster. The idea was to take everything possible off of the motorcycle so it would be lighter, go faster, and win races. If a part was not essential to the function of the motorcycle, it was taken off. Front fenders were often taken off completely and rear fenders were bobbed, or cut back to the bare minimum— hence the name "bobber" for a stripped-down Harley. Then guys started designing their own parts to make their bikes look unique. In fact, the first aftermarket part famous bike builder Arlen Ness created was a set of custom handlebars.

In the early 1950s, the world of outlaw motorcycle clubs and motorcycle customizing was still in its infancy, but both would soon learn to walk and then run with amazing speed all across the country. After the AMA announcement that the trouble-making element in motorcycling only amounted to 1 percent of the riding population, it wasn't long before a diamond-shaped patch began to appear on cutoff denims and leathers. The diamond one percenter patch is a badge of honor to those outsiders spurned by society. Bikers wearing a one percenter patch are serious about their club. Putting on leathers is not a fashion show for these men, and riding is not a weekend pastime; it's truly a way of life.

Stanley Kramer's 1954 film *The Wild One* helped foster the image of the modern outlaw biker and a lot of young guys wanted to be cool like Marlon Brando's character, Johnny Stabler. Plus, as the old saying goes, "Ladies love outlaws," and the image of the black leather-clad hellion on a loud motorcycle was just the bad boy image to draw girls who were looking to be a little bit bad themselves.

By the early 1960s, motorcycle clubs had sprouted up all across America, but southern California again led the way and there have been many righteous outlaw motorcycle clubs in California over the years.

The style of bike changed dramatically during this period. Not content to simply cut parts off their motorcycles, bikers began building their own frames, tanks, and fenders. Custom paint got wilder and extended front ends got longer and crazier. Apehanger

The good ol' boy vets clubs,
such as the Boozefighters,
had made way for the darker
vision of greasy long-haired
one percenters in "originals"
(jeans so encrusted with motor
oil they could stand
up on their own).

handlebars reached for the stars, as did long, chromed exhaust pipes with fishtails on the ends. Choppers exploded on the SoCal scene with their king and queen seats and psychedelic paint jobs.

Meanwhile, the Woodstock generation was tuning in and dropping out; beat poets and antiwar demonstrations went hand in hand with flower power, free love, and hippies. But the good ol' boy vets clubs, such as the Boozefighters, had made way for the darker vision of greasy long-haired one percenters in "originals" (jeans so encrusted with motor oil they could stand up on their own).

FROM A WILD ONE TO AN EASY RIDER

Chopper-riding long hairs were the perfect bad guys in any number of low-budget exploitation films in the late 1960s and early 1970s, and most of these were made in southern California. Of all the low-dough moviemakers of that time period, two stand out as being at the top of the heap: Samuel Z. Arkoff and Roger Corman. Arkoff's American International Pictures (AIP) produced everything from cheesy monster movies, such as *I Was a Teenage Werewolf*, to the *Beach Blanket* films, along with about a dozen low-budget biker films, including the now classic *The Wild Angels*, *Angels from Hell*, *The Devil's Angels*, *Born Losers*, and others. Producer/director Roger Corman had worked with Arkoff on AIP's *Attack of the Crab Monsters* and other B-horror movies. In 1966, Hunter S. Thompson's book,

Hell's Angels: The Strange and Terrible Saga of the Outlaw Motorcycle Gangs, was a hot seller with its inside look at the Oakland chapter of the Hells Angels. Corman was inspired by Thompson's book as well as a picture in *Life* magazine that showed a long line of outlaw bikers attending a biker funeral in California for one of their fallen brothers. Corman got together with veteran screenwriter Charles Griffin and, based on that photo and a smattering of information from Thompson's book, created the screenplay for *The Wild Angels.*

In the late 1960s the media circus surrounding outlaw bikers was just beginning and *The Wild Angels* only added fuel to the fire. It seemed that the world had a strange fascination with one per-centers. Seeing the amazing spectacle of a pack of bikers blasting down the highway on choppers or roaring en masse up Pacific Coast Highway is a sight that burns its way into your memory forever. I've heard more stories than I can count of young guys seeing a swarm

"We'd like to award you this booze. After all, you can't be a Boozefighter without having the booze to fight over."

of one percenters thundering along together that caused a lasting impression and a lifelong love affair with motorcycles.

Because *The Wild Angels* was a hit at drive-ins and so was the 1969 film *Easy Rider*, American B-movie makers quickly produced a slew of really lousy films. AIP got to work on a dozen different iron horse operas. Of these films, *The Devil's Angels* (1967) stands out as a particularly revealing foray into the underbelly of bikerdom. In it, director Daniel Haller basically strings together every outlaw biker cliché then known into a mishmash of brawls, booze, and badass bikes, starring John Cassavetes. The fictitious MC club The Skulls spend a lot of time swilling brew and riding their scoots, and they apparently have a penchant for demolishing recreational vehicles. The infamous Hells Angels Monterey rape trial was going on when this flick came out, and it was sure to mimic and exploit such perversion with scenes of leering Skulls being accused of raping a whole town full of young ladies.

In classic western tradition, the bad guy bikers are driven out of town by the local lawmen but are then attacked by a bunch of rednecks. What comes across is some of the *feeling* of being in an outlaw club without any of the substance. The Skulls are seen as a tribe of wandering vagrants who ride their bikes in formation like some guerilla military group, sworn to fun and loyal to none.

Other cheap biker movies followed, such as *The Glory Stompers*, *Rebel Rousers*, *Born Losers*, and *The Cycle Savages*, and each added to the myth of the one percenter. These movies were not just about motorcycle clubs invading small towns. Once in a while, some of

> Seeing the amazing spectacle of a pack of bikers blasting down the highway on choppers or roaring en masse up Pacific Coast Highway is a sight that burns its way into your memory forever.

these movies actually included biting social commentary. Such was the case in *The Savage Seven*. Popular for his work in B-movies, Adam Rourke starred as the MC club leader, reprising his role from *Hell's Angels on Wheels*. In *The Savage Seven*, Rourke and his club fight to defend a Native American girl from redneck bigots. The club discovers that they have a lot in common with the Indians, since both groups are seen as outcasts in American society.

In *Angels from Hell*, a Vietnam vet named Mike, played by Tom Stern, returns from war and looks up his old bike club The Mad Caps, only to find that they were run out of town by the local sheriff. Mike gets pissed and decides to create a worldwide club that will go head to head with the cops. Alas, Mike can't even keep his own small club together.

In a parody of the kind of media coverage that propelled the Hells Angels to stardom, the Fanfare Films production of *Run, Angel, Run* starred William Smith as the member of the Devil's Advocates Motorcycle Club. Smith sells a story about the club he's in to a national magazine and gets his face on the cover. This doesn't sit well with the club, however, and Smith has to, well . . . run, Angel, run!

One of the more popular biker movies of the time was *C.C. and Company*, starring NFL football star Joe Namath and the sultry Ann-Margret up against bad guy biker William Smith. While the film is big on star power, it is shy on plot, although the smoking-hot Ann-Margret nude scene goes a long way toward absolving the film-makers of that particular sin. A much more entertaining film is *Hells Angels '69*, starring actual members of the Hells Angels, including Sonny Barger and the fun-to-watch Terry the Tramp. The bank heist plot line is pretty silly, but the Angels look good roaring down the California and Nevada highways.

Still other biker movies that tried to cash in on the media blitz of evil biker articles included *The Losers*, *Angel Unchained*, and *Bury Me an Angel*. But none of the slew of cycle cinema could capture the big bucks at the box office of, nor the style and sense of freedom found in, *Easy Rider*.

In that film, Captain America, as played by Peter Fonda, with his red, white, and blue stars and stripes panhead chopper, is the quiet reminder of what this country stands for. He is liberty. Dennis Hopper's character of Billy (as in Billy the Kid) on his flame-painted

There is something about watching choppers float down southwestern highways in the glory of golden-hour light that touches on the freedom you feel when piloting a big V-twin.

chopper is the ugly American, the frontiersman with his pushy ways and rebellious spirit. They are America incarnate as they roll across this country looking for themselves and a bit of the American Dream. As the advertising slogan for the film read, "A man went looking for America and couldn't find it anywhere."

There has never been a biker film before or after *Easy Rider* that has captured the essence of what riding is all about as well as this film does. There is something about watching those choppers float down southwestern highways in the glory of golden-hour light that touches on the freedom you feel when piloting a big V-twin. Indeed, in the year following the release of the film, Americans bought motorcycles in record numbers. We all wanted a little bit of that freedom.

THE BADDEST OF THE BAD

Thanks in part to exploitation biker films, one percenters became easy prey when Hollywood was looking for bad guys in their modern-day horse operas (with motorcycles taking the place of horses). Most of these California-based films truly are westerns, right down to the borrowed plots. At the same time, real outlaw bikers had become true nonconformists and distanced themselves from the straight-laced citizenry by becoming the antithesis of the image of the white-shirted, churchgoing good guy. Bikers wanted to be bad to the bone, and one percenters became the baddest of the bad. Still, there is much more than meets the eye when examining the image of the one percenter.

One percenters are an extension of the outlaw spirit of the American West, and the One Percenter Code is very much the Code of the West. Think about it. Bikers are modern-day cowboys and frontiersmen, living life on their own terms. Bikers relate to the characters Clint Eastwood has played in westerns, especially the laconic antihero he played in Italian westerns, because they, like his "man with no name," are also antiheroes in our society.

The One Percenter Code has much in common with the Code of the West, and like that fabled code of cowboys in the American West, no definitive written One Percenter Code exists. Many believe that the Code of the West is based on the novel by the same name penned by Zane Grey in 1934, but the rules of the code actually go back long before that. At the heart of the code are the simple instructions: If it's not yours, don't take it; if it's not true, don't say it; if it's not right, don't do it. This goes hand in hand with "A cowboy's word is his sacred bond."

Famous for starring in many classic western films, John Wayne said of cowboys, "They were simple, direct men. They believed in things like liberty and minding their own business. When the first

Oh give me a home where the buffalo roam and the rowdy ol' bikers all play.

cowboys were herding longhorns up the Chisholm Trail from Texas to Kansas, they were a pretty tough lot, but they had to be. It was a rough era in our history. There was no room for nuance or no time for luxury."

THE CODE OF THE WEST

In the last chapter, I asked a number of hardcore bikers to try to put into words a suggested code of conduct to live by. I asked the same thing of a number of men out West who still honor and live by the cowboy's Code of the West. You'll notice that many of their rules are the same as the Code of Chivalry used by the knights of old and are remarkably similar to the ideals of the One Percenter Code. Here is what you might call the cowboy's way:

· Be loyal.
· Live each day with courage.
· Assist others in need.
· A deal sealed with a handshake is more binding than any legal documents.
· Lay down your life, if necessary, for the privilege of defending your outfit (or bike club).
· Endure hardships without complaining.
· Take pride in your work.
· Never tolerate a coward.
· Talk less and say more.
· Don't make excuses.
· Always finish what you start and never quit.
· Always keep a promise.
· Be generous with your life and money.
· Be tough but fair.
· Know where to draw the line.
· Treat women like ladies.
· Never shoot an unarmed or unwarned man.

When I was a kid, westerns were incredibly popular, especially among us little whippersnappers. Books about the Old West were a

Cowboys have their rodeos, and bikers have the
Easyriders Motorcycle Rodeo.

lot of fun to read, there were radio shows devoted to westerns, and
even western adventures on the new-fangled thing called television.
I loved watching Roy Rogers sing and shoot his way through the
West and I think that a lot of what I remember as being a code to
live by came from cowboy stars like Roy Rogers and Dale Evans, the
Lone Ranger, and Gene Autry.

Known as the singing cowboy, Gene is best known today for his hit
single "Rudolph the Red-Nosed Reineer." From 1940 to 1956, Autry
had a weekly radio show on CBS Radio called *Gene Autry's Melody
Ranch*. He created the Cowboy Code, or Cowboy Commandments, in
response to his young radio listeners aspiring to emulate him. Here
is Gene Autry's code:

- The cowboy must never shoot first, hit a smaller man, or take
  unfair advantage.
- He must never go back on his word or betray a trust confided
  in him.
- He must always tell the truth.
- He must be gentle with children, the elderly, and animals.
- He must not advocate or possess racially or religiously
  intolerant ideas.

- He must help people in distress.
- He must be a good worker.
- He must keep himself clean in thought, speech, action, and personal habits.
- He must respect women, parents, and his nation's laws.
- The cowboy is a patriot.

Believe it or not, there is a Center for Cowboy Ethics and Leadership and under the heading "Why Cowboys?" on its website (www.cowboyethics.org), the following can be found:

> What kind of person does it take to get up in the middle of the night, saddle up his horse and set out into a raging blizzard, all to rescue a calf he doesn't even own? This cowboy is simply "doing what has to be done" with no regard for his own comfort or safety.
>
> But remember, you don't have to do extraordinary deeds to be a hero. Cowboys are heroic, not just because they do a dangerous job, but because they stand for something. Principles like honor, loyalty and courage are at the heart of the Cowboy Way.
>
> Even though cowboy life has changed over the past 150 years, cowboys still honor and live by their code. They are a source of inspiration that reaches back into our history, yet still speaks to us today. At a time when heroes are in short supply, cowboys are the real deal.

A group called the Paragon Foundation even publishes a magazine called *The Cowboy Way* that is filled with entertaining stories that celebrate rural values and the culture of the American West, while educating and empowering citizens regarding their constitutional rights. Its mission statement extols constitutional principles, individual freedoms, private property rights, and the continuation of rural customs and culture—all with the intent of celebrating and continuing our founding fathers' vision for America. Sounds like every biker I know would get behind that.

Ultimately, the Code of the West was composed of whatever a man said it was. While some of the noblest deeds of the Old West were performed in the name of the code, it also accounted for some

While there are outlaw motorcycle clubs all over the planet, the origin of the leather-clad, longhaired rider astride a thundering chopper is a very American concept, and the image of the one percenter is definitely connected to cowboys, gunslinging outlaws, and Pony Express riders of old.

mighty sordid acts as well. Since there was very little law in the West, men made their own rules to live by. Some of the cardinal principles of the Code of the West involve the contractual bond of a man's word, death to all horse thieves, and hospitality to strangers. At its simplest, the code offered a common ethic for fair play.

Whether the modern-day one percenter knows it or not, many of the rules of the road that he lives by might just have taken root from our ideas of the ol' Code of the West and the cowboy way. There is a very real kinship between bikers and the Wild West outlaws that we should explore.

While there are outlaw motorcycle clubs all over the planet, the origin of the leather-clad, longhaired rider astride a thundering chopper is a very American concept, and the image of the one per-center is definitely connected to cowboys, gunslinging outlaws, and Pony Express riders of old.

The story of the American Wild West is rich with a very diverse cast of interesting characters that all inspired the modern image of the outlaw biker. Rugged mountain men, such as Kit Carson and Jim Bridger, and pistol-packin' legends, such as Buffalo Bill Cody and Annie Oakley, stir the imagination with their legendary stories of taming the great unknown American West. True Wild West bad boys and outlaws, such as Jesse James and Billy the Kid, light the

Bikers look and act like bikers all over the world. These bros are from Denmark.

fires of rebellion in the heart of the tribe that would become known as bikers. The true-life legends that inspired the fiction of penny dreadfuls, dime-store novels, and western shoot 'em up movies all breathed life into the biker image.

Westerns deal with the conquest of the great American wilderness. The heroes of westerns generally adhere to codes of honor rather than to strict interpretations of the law. The classic western movie usually follows the story of a lone man on a horse as he struggles to do the right thing in a land known for its independence and freedom from oppression.

Many of the biker lifestyle paintings of *Easyriders* magazine artist David Mann famously showed the link between bikers and their Wild West counterparts. Because of the untamed spirit of the Pony Express rider, David created what was perhaps his most popular painting as a centerspread for *Easyriders* (November 1983) that featured a Pony Express rider. The painting is called *Ghostrider* and shows a wild and free biker with tattooed arms, blasting down a stretch of desert highway on his faithful rigid-framed shovelhead. To his left, pacing him, is the ghost of the Pony Express rider. The message is clear: The spirit of the biker and the Wild West rider are one and the same.

THE RED AND WHITE

Some of the most revered motorcycle clubs in the world began in southern California, but the best-known one percenter club without a doubt has to be the Hells Angels, not just because The Red and White started in California, but because of their high-profile history, the media coverage that turned the club into a household name, and the fact that there have been a slew of exploitation films based on them.

According to Sonny Barger, former president of the Oakland chapter of the Hells Angels and one of the most highly regarded members of the club, a group of bikers were riding around Oakland, California, wearing the death's head patch and calling themselves Hells Angels back in 1957. But they found out that there were two other clubs in California using the same logo and

The remnants of the Pissed Off Bastards changed their name to the Hells Angels after the Hollister incident in 1948.

The Hells Angels are said to have more than 60 chapters in North America and nearly 40 in other countries.

calling themselves the same thing. One of the clubs was from San Bernadino, the remnants of the Pissed Off Bastards who, after the Hollister incident, changed their name to the Hells Angels in 1948. This chapter is generally thought to have been the first chapter of The Red and White.

In his book *Let's Ride*, Sonny describes how he learned about the other chapters of the club:

> In 1958 I rode with a guy named Ernie Brown, who was the vice president of the club I was in at the time. We'd ridden down to Los Angeles and my transmission blew up. We were sitting on the side of the road when another motorcyclist named Vic Bettencourt stopped to help. It turned out that he was the president of a chapter of the same club.
>
> I didn't even know our club had a chapter down there. We'd founded our club because we'd found a cool patch from a defunct club and we liked the patch. We didn't even know there were other chapters of the club. It was the first time we realized we were part of something bigger than just the club my friends and I had started. Vic took us to their clubhouse and put a new transmission in my bike. He also taught me a lot about what brotherhood was all about.

The Hells Angels incorporated in 1966 being "dedicated to the promotion and advancement of motorcycle riding, motorcycle clubs, motorcycle highway safety, and all phases of motorcycling and motorcycle driving." The club trademarked their "death's head" logo in 1972 and their name in the 1980s. Now, the Hells Angels are said to have more than 60 chapters in North America and nearly 40 in other countries.

AN AMERICAN ORIGINAL

In recent years, the One Percenter Code and the way of life envisioned by the Hells Angels has been the thinly disguised inspiration for the hit TV series *Sons of Anarchy*. The show takes place in the fictional town of Charming, California, where a notorious outlaw motorcycle club protects its livelihood at all costs. According to FX Network, "The MC must confront threats from drug dealers,

Chances are this guy always finishes what he starts.

corporate developers, and overzealous law officers. Behind the MC's familial lifestyle and legally thriving automotive shop is a ruthless and illegally thriving arms business."

Like the Hells Angels, the fictional Sons of Anarchy have chapters all over the world, but in the series the focus is on the founding chapter known as Sons of Anarchy Motorcycle Club, Redwood Original, or SAMCRO. The club's president, Clay Morrow (played by Ron Perlman), protects the small town of Charming at all costs.

While series creator Kurt Sutter says the storyline of *Sons of Anarchy* is based on Shakespeare's *Hamlet*, it is also just a stone's throw away from the real world of former Hells Angels president Sonny Barger, known to his brothers as "Chief." *Sons of Anarchy* takes place in Charming, California, and Sonny is currently a member of the Cave Creek, Arizona, chapter of the Hells Angels, living in a small town called Lake Pleasant. Coincidence? Not according to Sutter, who spent time with Sonny when researching the idea for the series. Sonny also appeared in the season three finale of the show opposite Sutter in 2010. Talk about life imitating art, imitating life.

Watching an episode of *Sons of Anarchy*, you can't help but see the connection to the western genre. Those flat, endless desert vistas, cacti, and sagebrushes all seem to be pulled from a Louis L'Amour western story. A small western town under the protection of a strong man and his family. The familiar tale of a man, a horse, and a gun . . . only the horse is a Harley-Davidson. A similar two-wheeled western TV series, *Renegade*, rode the airwaves a few years ago starring Lorenzo Lamas as a bounty hunter on the run from the law.

Outlaw bikers are as iconic as the great Indian chiefs who toured the country in Buffalo Bill Cody's Wild West Shows more than 100 years ago, and people today will line up to meet a real one per-center. Look at Sonny Barger. He has been riding motorcycles for more than 50 years and has been in a motorcycle club for almost as long. In the world of bikers, he's a god. As previously mentioned, Sonny has appeared in such films as *Hells Angels on Wheels* and *Hell's Angels '69* and has written such books as *Hell's Angel: The Life and Times of Sonny Barger and the Hell's Angels Motorcycle Club*, *Freedom: Credos from the Road*, *Dead in 5 Heartbeats*, and *6 Chambers, 1 Bullet*. He was editor for the book *Ridin' High, Livin' Free* and recently wrote *Let's Ride: Sonny Barger's Guide to Motorcycling* with Darwin Holmstrom, the editor for the book you are holding.

In his book *Freedom: Credos from the Road*, Sonny talks about his own One Percenter Code and the principles he lives by. He has had one helluva wild ride of a life, some would say a tough life, and he is a survivor. He mentions that motorcycles don't have a reverse gear, and that in life, like in riding a motorcycle, you have to keep moving forward. He also says that few make it to the top by being ordinary: "Originals don't come off an assembly line." I like that and he's right as far as I'm concerned.

In an interview about his book *Freedom*, he was quoted as saying, "If you lie down and let somebody kick you, you're never going to get nowhere. You have to stand up. It's not like being out there and being a bully and just jumping on everybody because you want to do it or because you're able to do it, but you can't lie down when people come on to use you; you have to stand up for your rights, too."

In a society of plastic people without any heart or breath or soul, Sonny is a true original and a true one percenter, a man who lives by his own code.

A COUNTRY IN NEED OF A GOOD THUMPIN'

People today need to learn that there are consequences for their actions. Children need to be taught this, but just as important is the fact that a lot of people in this country feel entitled. They feel entitled to a McMansion and a smart phone and a desk job and

> One percenters are happy to teach disrespectful pieces of shit lessons about life.

a $5,000 suit, just like all the yuppies they see in movies and on TV. These are people who have never been beaten up. These are people who didn't get their beatings to teach them to have a little respect for others.

A friend of mine—lifelong biker, custom painter, and magazine editor Crazy John Gilbert—would always comment when he came across a particularly rude or too-big-for-his-britches hombre, "That guy never got his beating." Now I'm not telling you to beat your kids or anything like that, but I am in favor of instilling a sense of responsibility in kids—hell, in everyone!

We live in a very litigious country in which everybody is out to sue everybody else. Remember the lady who sued a fast-food chain because she burned her hand on some hot coffee she bought there? What the hell? Wouldn't she be pissed if the coffee was cold? What about personal responsibility? What about saying, "My bad, the coffee was hot and I burned myself because I'm an idiot." But noooooo! This dingbat can't take a little responsibility for her actions.

The thing is we see this sort of bullshit every day, from the idiot who slips and falls on the sidewalk and sues the homeowner for not spraying his driveway with some sort of adhesive to keep his sneakers stuck to the pavement, to every single thing corporations and our government officials do, proceeding through the lens that we all need a couple hundred vultures in lawyer suits to protect us from getting sued because no one will take any gawd-damned responsibility for their actions.

Well, guess what? One percenters don't wait to call their lawyers to straighten things out, so you had better learn that there are consequences for your actions and you better start being responsible. One percenters are happy to teach disrespectful pieces of shit lessons about life.

After decades of being overindulged, this country has become a spoiled brat and you know what they say about sparing the rod. Maybe a good thumping would help straighten things out. This country needs a good thumping. Just think of it this way: What would John Wayne do?

5.
ONE PERCENTER ETIQUETTE

WHEREIN WE LEARN HOW TO RUN WITH WOLVES AND HOW TO EARN AND GIVE RESPECT IN THE BIKER WORLD

> "Have you ever tried to pick up your bloody teeth off the ground with a broken hand?"
>
> —Gary Creekmore, one percenter

NOW it's time to get to the nitty-gritty. Thanks for staying with me so far on this journey and for being patient. It is time to delve into the world of the one percenter from the point of view of both a civilian and as a fully patched member.

Walking into a biker bar is a lot like going back in time to stroll into a saloon in the Old West. Imagine this scenario: Let's say you are a member of a small motorcycle club. You walk into the bar and a couple of one percenters are there already. There are three of 'em over at a private table wearing their leathers and cuts, and their patches show them to be fully patched members. What should you do? The One Percenter Code tells us to always walk up to the patch holders and present yourself, letting them know who you are and who you ride with out of respect for their patch. Offering to buy them a round is a good idea too. But make sure not to interrupt them if they are talking. Stand at a respectful distance and wait for them to finish their conversation. If they ignore you after a minute, just nod and keep walkin'.

If you're in the bar first, having a drink, and the one percenters saunter in, the same rules apply. Walk up and introduce yourself as a way of showing their colors some respect. Respect is a big deal to one percenters. How do you know to do all this? Because you have been carefully schooled by your club brothers and other members of the motorcycle community (and, hopefully, by this book) and know that you always show respect to any prospect or full patch holder (PH) of a one percenter motorcycle club.

THE PARABLE OF THE BEER AND THE PATCH

Here's a true story. A friend of mine (we'll call him Bill, but that's not his name) has grown up around motorcycles, and his father and older brother are respected members of a major one percenter motorcycle club. Bill rides and enjoys the biker lifestyle to the hilt, but he has never wanted to join a one percenter club because of all the rules and regulations and because one percenters are just too intense and serious about club matters for his liking. He's an easygoing guy and it's just not his thing.

Though his father has asked him to join the club several times, Bill always politely turned down the offers. "I went to the clubhouse exactly one time," Bill says. "It was my first and last time ever going into a one percenter clubhouse."

His father and brother were at the clubhouse for a big club party and everything was going swell. Bill had a full beer in his hand and as he was walking past a patch holder, someone accidentally bumped Bill's arm and the beer spilled on the PH's cut and club patch. If you just said, "Oh *shit*!" you're right. You *never* touch a one percenter. You never touch his cut or his patch, even if you are friends. Nothing is more sacred to a one percenter than his patch, and touching it,

> Nothing is more sacred to a one percenter than his patch, and touching it, and for god's sake, *spilling* something on it, is considered to be disrespectful in the extreme.

Despite appearances, bikers are your neighbors, your local businessmen, and sometimes even the coaches of your Little League team.

and for god's sake, *spilling* something on it, is considered to be disrespectful in the extreme.

Bill tried his best to apologize to the PH, buy him a beer, put things right, but in the one percenter world, "Honor must be paid." That means a thumpin' is coming. The PH began yelling at Bill and pulled a knife. Bill's father and brother stepped in and, being that Bill's father was very high up and respected in the club, everyone quieted down.

By the code of the one percenters, the two men had to take it outside and settle their beef. Bill's father told all present that the two should fight one on one with no club members jumping into the fight and that if anyone did jump in, they would have to answer to him.

Bill went outside and proceeded to knock the living shit out of the patch holder. So much so that his brother had to pull him off of the dude, knowing that if he kept kicking his ass, the entire club would pile in on Bill, enforcing the one percenter rule "You fuck with one, you fuck with all." You can never provoke a club member without having to answer to the entire club. Once the fight was over and honor was served, the patch holder never mentioned the incident again. It was a done deal for the PH and the club, but Bill never set foot in the clubhouse again.

So if you are an outsider looking inside the outlaw biker world, how do you know how not to mess up and get yourself in deep trouble without even knowing what the hell you did to bring down the wrath of a one percenter motorcycle club on your delicate head? Ah, grasshopper, we are here to enlighten you.

RESPECT, PART II

One percenter motorcycle clubs are about earning and giving respect. They are about commitment and loyalty. Sure, members can be intimidating, but they are people just like you or me. They are your neighbors, your local businessmen, and sometimes even the coaches of your local Little League team. One percenters have wives and kids; some even go to church on Sundays. But being members of one percenter motorcycle clubs, they are loyal to their club brothers and passionate about their clubs and the biker lifestyle. They honor and protect each other because no one else will.

As the story related earlier shows, it can be easy to step into a situation and bring a world of hurt down on your head without even knowing what you did or how you offended the one percenter. What follows is a helpful list of things you should never do if you are a

Never touch a one percenter's motorcycle. It is his most highly prized possession.

civilian or involved in a riding club (such as Harley Owners Group members) when in close proximity of one percenters:

- As mentioned earlier, never touch a one percenter. Never touch a one percenter's cut or patch. Even brushing by in a crowded room could get you beat up.
- Never touch a one percenter's motorcycle unless you enjoy getting yourself a proper beating. Make sure your girlfriend never touches or sits on anyone's bike but your own.
- Don't drop names about who you know or think you know in a one percenter motorcycle club. You never know who might be listening and might take offense. Never spread gossip about a club.
- Don't call a one percenter *brother* or *bro* unless you deserve that privilege. Unless he really is your genetic brother or you are a fully patched member of the same club, this will get you socked up real quick.
- Don't think wearing a support shirt buys you anything. You are not a member; you are a civilian. Never wear a support shirt anywhere that a warring club can see it, or you are dead meat.
- Never say anything bad or disrespectful to a club member about one of his club brothers. Even if he agrees with you, you will still probably get thumped.
- Keep your thoughts to yourself. Until you show yourself as being about something and not one of the walking dead, one percenters don't give a shit what you think.
- *Never* disrespect a one percenter's ol' lady (girlfriend or wife). Period.
- When riding your motorcycle, never pull into a pack of one percenters traveling together like you are one of them. Stay out of the pack.
- Never interrupt two or more patch holders when they are having a conversation. This is disrespectful.
- Never take a photo of a one percenter. Even professional photographers for motorcycle magazines ask permission to take pictures of patch holders before snapping a flick.
- When one percenters are parked together, do not think that you can join their group and park next to them. Remember, you are a civilian to the club, even if you ride with the infamous Wild Hogs.

- But remember, the most important rule when dealing with one percenters is that you generally get what you give: Give respect and you will get respect back. However, if you disrespect a member or his club, there will be hell to pay.

UNCOMMON SENSE

Okay civilians, got all that? You might think that most of the rules listed earlier are just good common sense rules, such as "Never stick your hand in a lion's mouth," but you'd be surprised how many civilians and even members of riding clubs just wander up to a one percenter and do something really stupid. As Kim Peterson, the longtime editor of *In the Wind* magazine (and photographer for this book) says, "These days common sense ain't so common and neither is doing the right thing." Amen to that.

The main thing to remember is that a member of a one percenter motorcycle club not only "lives to ride and rides to live," but his club and his motorcycle are the most important things in his life, right up there with his blood relatives and his wife and kids. You always

One percenters come out to party just like the rest of us. But never disrespect a patch holder anywhere or at any time.

> "These days common sense ain't so common and neither is doing the right thing."

want to show one percenters the respect they deserve because the patch on their back is a symbol of the deep commitment and self-discipline each man had to demonstrate in order to wear that patch. It is a badge of honor, courage, and integrity.

Patch holders are schooled by the club on how to handle civilians, especially in public situations. They know that the walking dead out there don't know the rules, so they do generally cut folks some slack. You may have noticed this at motorcycle charity events when a club is participating and trying to raise money for a good cause. The members of the club try to be respectful of the public and not come off as being too scary or end up thumpin' some guy for being a lame asshole.

Motorcycle clubs of all kinds work with local city governments and charity groups to promote a positive image of bikers to help undo the decades of negative media publicity foisted on the public that gave the impression that all bikers are bad guys. In my opinion, the finest one percenter motorcycle clubs are always cognizant of how their actions will affect not only the club's image in the biker community, but, more importantly, to the citizens out there. Serious club members always conduct themselves in a professional manner.

MCS AND RCS

The general public doesn't know the difference between seeing a doctor or lawyer wearing shiny new leathers and a big Harley Owners Group patch on his back (known as an RC for riding club) and a seasoned patch holder for the Sons of Silence (known as an MC for "motorcycle club"). To the average Joe, we are all scooter trash, and if one group does something to draw negative publicity and ends up on the 11 o'clock news, we're *all* bad.

If you ride a motorcycle, you need to be aware that your actions reflect on the entire motorcycle community. Generally speaking, one percenter MCs are very aware of this and tend to police their own to avoid negative publicity. This brings us to the differences exhibited by riding clubs as opposed to motorcycle clubs, specifically one percenter motorcycle clubs.

Both RCs and MCs strive to conduct themselves responsibly, returning common courtesy and respect when it is given, and there are some similarities between the two groups, but there is a much higher level of commitment in an MC. In both organizations you are taught to keep a positive attitude and to participate in all club activities and runs. While RCs have monthly meetings, MCs have church night (for members only) that can occur monthly or even weekly.

While RCs are always open to new riders to join them, MCs are very selective on who they let in to their organization and just how

Never interrupt one percenters who are having a conversation. Make your presence known and wait politely to speak.

> The general public doesn't
> know the difference between
> seeing a doctor or lawyer
> wearing shiny new leathers
> and a big Harley Owners
> Group patch on his back and
> a seasoned patch holder for
> the Sons of Silence.

far to let that person in (we'll talk about hang-arounds, prospects, and patch holders later). The MC member is taught to keep his distance and not get overly friendly with people outside of the club, especially if he runs across someone who is asking a lot of questions about the function of the club. This is none of any civilian's business. When someone outside the club has questions, they are referred to a patch holder or officer of the club for answers.

By the same token, RCs aren't out to hide anything; they're just riding clubs. There aren't too many rules or pressures put upon RC members. While MCs are secretive about the inner workings of their club, members strive to conduct themselves with honor and dignity, especially while out in public. MC members know that they are always being watched, both by the club's officers and by the world at large. As the old one percenter saying goes, "When we do right, no one remembers; when we do wrong, no one ever forgets."

When out in the world on a motorcycle run, both RCs and MCs stick together with their respective groups for safety. The difference is that RCs have little fear that one of their members will be in trouble if he walks away from the group to sightsee. Not so for MCs. Members are taught to always keep an eye on their brothers and to never let anyone wander off alone in an unsecured area. MCs watch their brothers' backs at all times.

No matter who you ride with, it is disrespectful to use the term "outlaw club" when speaking to anyone about an MC. Remember, these are motorcycle clubs, not outlaw clubs and not gangs. All patch holders, regardless of who they ride with, have earned your respect; give it to them. Also remember to never turn your back on a patch holder from another club, not out of fear of an ambush, but out of respect for his patch. Be courteous, respectful, and professional; remember always that you are the walking embodiment of your club.

Finally, a riding club patch is never referred to as "colors." RC members should not wear any kind of banner on their patch that denotes the location of their club (known as a chapter location bar), and they should especially never wear the square MC patch that tells the world they are in a motorcycle club. Generally speaking, the RC patch is purchased by the rider, not earned out of dedication, loyalty, and brotherhood as is an MC patch.

ONE PERCENTER 101

For those of you who are ready to run with wolves, what follows is good basic information about the process of joining a one percenter motorcycle club. First, know that it is not something that should be entered into lightly. Being the proud member of an MC is not like joining the Elks Club or the Jaycees. Neither is it like joining the Harley Owners Group, where you are an automatic member just by buying a new Harley.

The arduous process of becoming a one percenter is divided up into four steps:

1. Looking at a club
2. Becoming a hang-around
3. Becoming a prospect
4. Becoming a patch holder

The first step involves doing your homework on the club in question and attending several functions that are open to the public, such as motorcycle rallies, runs, charity events, and the like. If the MC handles itself in a way that is righteous according to your way of thinking, you go to step two: becoming what is known as a hang-around.

HANG-AROUND

One of the best ways to become a hang-around is to ride to places where you know the club hangs out and let them see you and check out what you're about.

If you already know a patch holder in the club, walk on over, but remember not to interrupt him if he is in a conversation with another member, and wait to be acknowledged. Never touch him or throw your arm around him like a buddy. Other members are watching, and a move toward one of their brothers that might be misconstrued as aggressive behavior will bring other members down on you. No, I'm not kidding.

Don't put your hand out to shake the PH's hand; wait until he offers his hand to you. As mentioned earlier, if the PH doesn't acknowledge you, just keep on walking; something may be up that doesn't concern you. If you need to speak with an officer in the club, proper protocol is to look up the sergeant-at-arms to put in your request.

Motorcycle clubs often have club functions that are open to other MCs and even the invited public. Attending such a function is a good way to check out the club and have members check you out. As you attend more club functions, you may be invited to join the club at its favorite watering hole or even its clubhouse. The process of inching your way into a MC is slow and tedious. Once you are considered a hang-around, you are still not a member or representative of the club and neither you nor the club has any claim on the other. If you run your mouth and end up in trouble with another club, the MC you are hanging with has no obligation to back you up. You are on your own, pilgrim.

The hang-around period is a time to really see what the club is all about up close and find out if being a member of an MC is really for you or not. The vast majority of hang-arounds do not become fully patched members. The club is also sizing you up and finding out what you are about and if you have the right stuff to be a brother. At this point you can walk away from the club and visa versa, no hard feelings, kind of like going out on a date to see if you want to go out on a second date.

If you are a hang-around for a club, *do not* hang around any other motorcycle club. This is not like a dating service or motorcycle

> The hang-around period is
> a time to really see what
> the club is all about up close
> and find out if being a member
> of an MC is really for
> you or not.

buffet. MCs are looking for loyalty and honor in those who choose to ride with them; hanging with another club at this phase would show great disloyalty and disrespect for the club.

Should you decide that going any further with the club is not for you, there is a protocol for stepping away honorably with due respect to the club and its patch. If a patch holder is sponsoring you into the club, go to him and tell him that you want out. Then together the two of you will let the club president (the "P") know of your decision.

If you end up wanting to prospect for a club and members think you might have what it takes to ride with them, you may be asked to prospect and a patch holder will sponsor you. If so, your life is about to change because you will enter the "biker boot camp" phase of your journey toward being a one percenter.

PROSPECT

Lucky you, you have the honor of being a foot soldier for the biker nation, and like any soldier, the training period is intense and designed to test your mettle. As a prospect you may be at the bottom of the MC food chain, but you will be tempered by fire and forged into a mighty sword.

First thing's first—before you put on that cut with the "prospect" patch on the back, remember this at all times: Never, ever discuss the club or its business with anyone, period. Seems simple, doesn't it? Yet how many prospects have opened their yaps and found themselves on the outs before they knew what hit 'em? Silence makes for a happy life. Got it?

A motorcycle club is an organization of like-minded individuals who happen to live, eat, and breathe motorcycles, but it is first and foremost a brotherhood. Get to know all the brothers in the club, learn their names and road names (nicknames), talk to each of them about their jobs, their hobbies, and their families. But even more importantly, be there for your club brothers no matter what, no matter when. If a brother calls you and is broken down on the freeway at four in the morning, get your ass out of bed and go save his ass.

Prospects attend all club events and must do as they are told by patch holders, no questions asked. As low man on the totem pole, if asked, you must stay outside in the pouring rain watching the club's motorcycles while the rest of the club is inside a bar or the clubhouse partying the night away. Never let a PH hold an empty drink; cart away the dead soldier and place a fresh one in his hand. Never let a member of the club go anywhere alone and watch your brothers' backs. Prospecting is a labor of love for the club, and the better job you do to show that you really give a shit about the club and all it stands for, the better chance you have of becoming a patch holder.

Motorcycle clubs of all kinds work with local
city governments and charity groups to promote
a positive image of bikers.

The prospecting period can be different for each MC, but you generally have to prospect for at least a year for the following reasons:

The club needs to see how you handle yourself in any number of different situations.

As a prospect you are learning the One Percenter Code of conduct from other members, including MC etiquette and protocol.

You need to learn respect for the club, your brothers, and yourself.

You need to learn to participate in club functions.

You need to learn to ride with precision with your brothers.

The club needs to be sure beyond a shadow of a doubt that you have the right attitude to be a member of its elite organization.

PATCH HOLDER

O' happy day! You have earned your patch. After an initiation ceremony unlike any in the known world, you now stand with your brothers, proudly flying the club colors, showing the world that you are a true one percenter. Now you are allowed into the hallowed halls of church night with all the privileges afforded to a true club brother. From this point on in your life, you will become more strongly committed to the club and to the One Percenter Code.

Over time you will learn more about your brothers and become closer to them, having lived with them through thick and thin. You will know each club member's strengths and weaknesses and will have shared all of life's ups and downs together as a family.

CLUB BYLAWS

In Chapter One, I offered a composite list of club rules taken from many different one percenter clubs. Now that you know one percenters a little better, I'd like to show you a similar list of bylaws that apply to most one percenter motorcycle clubs. Technically, these clubs are nonprofit organizations that have an executive board,

> From this point on in your life, you will become more strongly committed to the club and to the One Percenter Code.

including a president, vice president, secretary, treasurer, road captain, and sergeant-at-arms.

PRESIDENT

The president's duties include the following:

1. To preside over meetings of both the executive board and the club
2. To judge items not covered in the constitution or in the rules and regulations
3. To act as the personal representative of the motorcycle club in the area of public relations, as a liaison between the MC and local law enforcement agencies, and as a connecting link between the MC and other motorcycle clubs
4. To represent the club in any business contacts and to supervise economic transactions
5. To assist MC officers in the interpretation of their club responsibilities and to promote club life among members

VICE PRESIDENT

The duties of the vice president are to assume the responsibilities of the president when he is unable to do so.

SECRETARY

The secretary's duties include the following:

1. To record and safeguard the minutes of the club meetings
2. To maintain the club constitution, recording any additions, deletions, or modifications
3. To handle any club correspondence

TREASURER

The treasurer's duties include the following:

1. To monitor and record the club's income and expenditures
2. To collect the dues and fines owed by members

ROAD CAPTAIN

The road captain's duties include the following:

1. To plan the travel routes and itinerary for club runs
2. To lead the club in formation while riding together
3. To enforce club rules and procedures for group riding

SERGEANT-AT-ARMS

The sergeant-at-arms' duties include the following:

1. To maintain order at club meetings and club activities
2. To ensure that members adhere to club rules, policies, and codes of conduct when dealing with other members or civilians
3. To defend club members, property, or territory from outside threats

ELECTION OF OFFICERS

Officers of the club usually serve 12-month terms of office, and annual elections are usually held at the last regular meeting of the year, in December. The following rules apply to most club officers:

1. In order to be eligible for office, a patch holder has to have been an active member in good standing for a minimum of one year.
2. Patch holders who aspire toward a particular position will campaign informally for one month prior to the elections.
3. Hopeful candidates will approach a member, inform them that he is willing to stand for office if nominated, ask for the member's opinion of his qualifications, and solicit the member's support.

CHURCH MEETINGS

Church almost always requires the presence of all patch holders who are eligible to vote on club matters. In general, the meetings follow these rules:

1. One organized meeting is held per month.
2. Majority rules.
3. If a vote is taken at a meeting and a member is not there, his vote is void.
4. Meetings will be closed except for prospective members and anyone there on business.
5. All meetings will be run on a parliamentary basis. Members will be evicted for unruly conduct.
6. Quorum for a meeting is 60 percent of membership and 80 percent for membership votes.
7. Everyone will attend the meeting on his bike during favorable weather, unless his bike is not running at the time. If the club calls a ride/meeting, all members will attend. If a member is working or sick, he will be excused. Members will be reprimanded if they repeatedly miss club functions.
8. Members must have colors with them when attending meetings.
9. Members must be straight during club meetings. They will be fined if they are drunk or fucked up.
10. There will be absolutely no booze or drugs consumed during meetings.
11. During a meeting, there will be no talking among members until they get the floor through the president. A sergeant-at-arms, if not present, will be appointed and anyone not abiding by the above will be evicted.
12. If a member misses three meetings in a row, he is out of the club.
13. If a member is thrown out of the club or quits without attending meetings, he loses his colors and anything he owns that has the club's colors, logos, or mottos on them. In some cases, this even includes club tattoos. How those tattoos are removed is a question best left unasked.

RULES REGARDING PROSPECTS
Most clubs use a version of the following rules regarding prospects:
1. A prospect must be at least 18 years old.

2. A prospect must own a Harley-Davidson (or other American-made) motorcycle.
3. A prospect cannot do any drugs.
4. A prospect must show a sincere interest in the motorcycle club and love bikes.
5. A prospect must have a functioning motorcycle equipped for the road.
6. A prospect must be sponsored by a patch holder who has known him at least one year.
7. The sponsor is responsible for the prospect.
8. The sponsor can pull a prospect's rockers at his discretion.
9. A prospect must attend all meetings and club functions.
10. A prospect must do anything a patch-holding club member tells him to do.
11. A prospect will stand behind the club and its members.
12. Prospects should not steal from members of the club.
13. A prospect must ride his bike to meetings.
14. Prospect members must be voted in. Two "no" votes equal a rejection. One "no" vote must be explained.
15. The prospecting period is at the discretion of the sponsor and the club.
16. Only the sponsor or an officer may hand out a patch to a prospect. This will be done at a meeting with only patch holders present.

Naturally, all motorcycle clubs differ on some points of their club rules, bylaws, and codes of conduct, but what I've shared with you in this chapter should give you the basic tools you'll need to survive when meeting a living, breathing wolf on two wheels. This has really only acted as an overview of some of the philosophy and structure of one percenter motorcycle clubs, and I am not suggesting that what I've written about in this chapter expresses the attitude or priorities of any specific motorcycle club.

If you are currently a member of a riding club, remember that even if you are trying to avoid contact with an outlaw motorcycle club, shit happens and it is better to be prepared. With that in mind, here are some basic rules for riding clubs when dealing with one percenters.

Tent cities like this spring up at all major
motorcycle rallies. You'd be surprised how spotless
this field will be when they leave.

RULES FOR RIDING CLUBS

Despite their fearsome image, one percenters are human beings
under all that leather. There are good and bad individuals in any
organization, and sometimes, no matter what you do to appease
someone, a patch holder's gonna be pissed off and there's nothing
you can do about it. However, if you keep your head, follow these
rules, and always give respect to one percenters, you'll live to ride
another day.

If a one percenter asks you who you ride with, answer politely
and give him your name (your real name, don't say, "Hiya, I'm Big
Razorback!"). Also give him the name of your club, let him know if
you are an officer in said club, and tell him where the club is from.
Don't offer to shake hands unless the one percenter offers his. If
he doesn't, don't make a big deal out of it. If you don't know the
answer to a question he asks, refer him to your club officers. Do not
make shit up. This will only piss him off.

> If asked, let the one
> percenter know that your
> club is nonterritorial and
> that no one in your club
> wears "support" patches
> or T-shirts.

A one percenter might ask you if your riding club has any intention of ever becoming a motorcycle club. The *only* answer to this question is "no." If asked, let the one percenter know that your club is nonterritorial and that no one in your club wears "support" patches or T-shirts. Your riding club is a nonterritorial, neutral club.

If you are in a riding club, then chances are very good that you welcome all makes and models of motorcycles, allow women in your club, and are an AMA-chartered club. These are three characteristics that are very seldom found in a one percenter motorcycle club, and such details let the MC know that your riding club is absolutely no threat. Some MC clubs allow motorcycles other than American-made (some one percenter clubs allow brands from countries that were allies during World War II, such as Great Britain and Russia), and the rare club does allow women as members, but *no* one percenter motorcycle club is ever a chartered member of the American Motorcycle Association.

Don't tell a patch holder how big your membership is or if there are other chapters of your riding club in other states. If the PH pushes for answers to these types of questions, refer him to one of the officers of your club. Also, patch holders don't always wear their colors, so be careful to not speak to anyone outside of your riding club about any interaction you have with a patch holder. You never know who might be listening and what tales might get back to the officers of the outlaw club. You don't want that.

Be careful where you choose to wear your riding club's patch because one percenter clubs are very territorial and some clubs don't see the difference between an RC and an MC, especially if they think you are moving in on their turf. If you are wearing your patch, be sure that it is when you are with a group of your fellow riders, never when you are alone. If you are going on a run and aren't sure which MCs are in the area you are traveling through and to, ask your club officers.

It is generally a bad idea to wear anything that might make you look like a member of a one percenter motorcycle club. This includes patches that are in any way similar to MC club colors, chapter location bars, or territory rockers across the bottom of your cut, or anything else that might confuse patch holders of MCs or the police. If cops think you're a member of some new MC they haven't heard of, you'll get the full "meet and greet" by the side of the road. They will run your bike and you, they will search your bike and you, and they will put a real damper on your day. Two words to remember: cavity search. 'Nuff said.

Let's say you and your riding club are out on the road, and you're all a bit parched and stop in at a biker-friendly bar only to find it full of one percenters. A patch holder comes over, checks you out, and asks you all to remove your vest with the cool patch on the back. The *only* correct response is "Yes, sir." Double likewise, remove your patch if asked when in the same situation all by your lonesome. Once you get back home, let your club officers know which MC you ran into just in case there are any miscommunications or problems down the road.

If you enter any establishment that has a "No Colors" sign on display, take your vest off. Even though you are in a riding club and not a member of an MC and your patch is not considered "colors," it is best to respect the wishes of the establishment as well as show respect to other clubs. After all, if there are MC members present who have honored the house rules and removed their cuts and you do not, they will be deeply offended. Establishments that have a "No Colors" policy generally do not distinguish between RCs and MCs; in other words, they don't know the difference between members of Wind & Fire (firefighters who ride), Douche Larouche (good-natured moto-jesters), and the Mongols (one percenters all the way). Get to know local hangouts that are friendly to motorcycle people and don't wear your RC patch unless they invite you to do so.

VISITING A CLUBHOUSE

Now let's say your riding club has been asked to join a party at a one percenter clubhouse and you decide to attend. First, do not wear your patch inside the clubhouse unless it has been approved by the MC in question. Second, do not talk to or bother any patch holder's ol' lady. Speak when spoken to. Third, there will be prospects running around fetching drinks for patch holders, getting them food, and generally serving as servants for the patch holders. Do not yell out, "Hey prospect! Get me a beer, will ya?" If you do, you'll notice that the place will get quiet real fast and all eyes will be on your dumb ass. You are a civilian, not a patch holder, and only patch holders can order prospects around. Always treat prospects with the same honor, courtesy, and respect you would reserve for patch holders.

When visiting an MC clubhouse, keep a good attitude and put that sparkling personality of yours to work. One of the quickest ways to get a well-deserved beating is to act like a disrespectful, macho asshole with a bad attitude. Make sure all members of your riding club know this and pull them outside if any of them get drunk and decide to start a fight or do something equally stupid. Remember

> Always treat prospects with the same honor, courtesy, and respect you would reserve for patch holders.

the One Percenter Code rule: "You fuck with one, you fuck with all." If one of your boys throws a punch, the whole MC will jump in and then you'll know what my ol' Diablo pal Gary Creekmore meant when he said, "Have you ever tried to pick up your bloody teeth off the ground with a broken hand?"

Last, but not least, as stated before, never touch a patch holder's cut or colors and never call a patch holder "brother" or "bro." Riding clubs and motorcycle clubs both live to ride and ride to live, but RCs are still made up of civilians, according to the one percenter world, and bike lover or not, you are not a one percenter's brother unless you have earned his respect by earning the colors of his club.

The One Percenter Code did not spring up overnight; it evolved over several hard-fought and hard-won decades and there are reasons for every rule.

6.

FROM A WILD ONE TO AN EASY RIDER

THE EVOLUTION OF THE OUTLAW BIKER LIFESTYLE AND ITS VARYING CODES OF CONDUCT

> "You know, this used to be a helluva good country. I can't understand what's gone wrong with it."
>
> —Jack Nicholson as George Hanson in *Easy Rider*

It seems as though any discussion of the One Percenter Code keeps coming back to biker films. There's a good reason for that — the public's perception of who and what bikers are all about has been forged by exploitation films in the 1950s, '60s, and '70s. For right or wrong, movies like *The Wild One, The Wild Angels*, and *Easy Rider* have left a lasting impression on our collective consciousness. In fact, one percenter motorcycle clubs in other parts of the world, especially in Europe and Australia, have based many of the aspects of their own One Percenter Code around these works of fiction.

Of all the examples of iron horse cinema, the film that became the ode to the Woodstock generation was definitely *Easy Rider*. In that 1969 film, speaking poetically on where we're all headed on what would become his last night on earth, George Hanson, played by Jack Nicholson, speaks his truth to Billy, played by Dennis Hopper. After George ponders whatever went wrong with America, Billy pipes up with, "Huh. Man, everybody got chicken, that's what's happened, man. Hey, we can't even get into, like, second-rate hotels. I mean, a second-rate hotel, man. They think we're gonna cut their throat or somethin'. They're scared, man."

George tells Billy, "Oh, they're not scared of you. They're scared of what you represent to them."

Billy laughs and says, "Hey man, all we represent to them, man, is somebody who needs a haircut."

One percenter motorcycle clubs in other parts of the world have based many of the aspects of their own One Percenter Code around the bike archetype created on film.

"Oh no," George smiles. "What you represent to them is freedom."

"What the hell's wrong with freedom, man? That's what it's all about," Billy insists.

"Oh yeah, that's right, that's what it's all about all right." George shakes his head. "But talking about it and being it, that's two different things. I mean it's real hard to be free when you are bought and sold in the marketplace. 'Course don't ever tell anybody that they're not free, 'cause then they're gonna get real busy killin' and maimin' to prove to you that they are. Oh yeah, they're gonna talk to you and talk to you about individual freedom, but when they see a free individual, it's gonna scare 'em."

"Yeah well, that don't make 'em running scared," Billy says.

George levels a burning gaze and says, "No, it makes 'em dangerous."

That night Nicholson's contemplative southern lawyer is killed by exactly the kind of redneck Americans he had just warned Billy about. The scene is downright scary for its sudden and deadly violence. From that moment on, the protagonists of the film are plunged into their dark night of the soul.

RUNNING OUT OF GAS

Easy Rider is filled with symbolism and deeper meaning for those who care to look for it, and there are definitely a few lessons fresh from the One Percenter Code peppered throughout the film. Producer and actor Peter Fonda has said that the movie is a contemporary western with choppers replacing horses, a sort of morality play for the gas-powered age. "It's not an accident that my character wears spurs on his boots in *Easy Rider*," Fonda says.

One of the running parables in *Easy Rider* has to do with being about something in this life. Throughout the film, Wyatt (Peter Fonda) and Billy meet many good, honest people trying to make it from the sweat of their brows and the strain of their backs. We see this when they meet the ranchers who help Wyatt fix a flat tire, and we see the members of the commune take the bikers in and feed them from their meager harvest. Do the bikers stop their drug-fueled cross-country sojourn aimed at retirement in Florida? No, they do not.

Again and again, we are shown that Wyatt and Billy are only interested in being consumers, making a big score and retiring. They are not about anything. In fact, the two characters are allegorical symbols of the American spirit and what is wrong with the American Dream. Captain America is the spirit of what this country was originally based upon. He is hope and the spirit of true freedom from

One percenters love to shatter stereotypes. George Christie, then-president of the Ventura, California, Hells Angels, prepares to run with the Olympic torch in 1984.

oppression, just as Billy represents the ugly American frontier spirit and the conscienceless masses yearning to consume Mother Earth without compassion. Captain America is Thomas Jefferson's concept of liberty, just as Billy represents the willingness to burn it all to the ground through mindless consumerism.

Billy thinks that freedom can be bought and sold in the marketplace. You score big and you're retired in Florida, mister. But Captain America keeps giving us clues in the film. When they break bread with the rancher, he tells his host, "It's not every man who can live off the land, you know? You do your own thing in your own time. You should be proud." Peter Fonda's character realizes toward the end of *Easy Rider* that he and Billy blew it because they stopped being about something and just concentrated on getting that gold watch, that brass ring.

If you take a look around you, you'll discover that there are far more Billys in this country today than Wyatts, and unchecked spending has led America to the brink of nationwide bankruptcy. As I write this, the country is trying to crawl out of the worst depression since the 1930s and the national debt has reached $14.3 trillion. For

Biker lifestyle artist David Mann (far right) captured the two-wheeled spirit in his paintings for *Easyriders* magazine.

> For the first time in history, America may default on its debt payments, and the rampant spending that some call the American Dream will turn into everyone's worst nightmare.

the first time in history, America may default on its debt payments, and the rampant spending that some call the American Dream will turn into everyone's worst nightmare.

Just as Wyatt and Billy took their cash and bought two-wheeled symbols of decadence and excess, we have become a country riding the highways on luxury wheels, cell phones in hand, talking to and texting everyone—a nation of idiots whose incessant babble signifies nothing. We've become a country without roots, without a tribe . . . lost. We're moving too fast to care about our neighbor, to raise a barn, to stop for a downed brother by the side of the road. We're all on the move, mindlessly racing toward that one big score so we can retire in Florida. We were born to sell out. Sadly, we're on a big highway in a shiny car that is out of gas and out of time.

YOU CAN KILL ME, BUT YOU CAN'T EAT ME

Many bikers today look back to watching films like *The Wild One* or *Easy Rider* when asked what first inspired them to start riding. Though the two films are miles and ages apart in their point of view, both show the biker as the hero or, more accurately, the antihero. Both films make you want to go out and kick-start a big Harley and twist the grip. Interestingly, both films warn that there is something very wrong going on in our country. For Johnny and his Black Rebels motorcycle club, life is a nonstop party and they're just having fun until the uptight town folk get all bent out of shape.

Peter Fonda reminds us that "We just want to be free to ride our machines without getting hassled by the Man," in *The Wild Angels*. And in *Easy Rider*, the two ex-carnies turned hippy bikers score big in a dope deal and ride their chromed-out choppers across America, only to get gunned down by rednecks. All these films are talking about the same thing: disenfranchised youth on the road to rebellion and the scared-stiff straight society that takes a moment out from going to church socials to lock the bikers up, shoot 'em, beat 'em, and blast 'em to hell. Looks like ol' George Hanson was right after all.

However, the moral lessons of *The Wild One*, *The Wild Angels*, and *Easy Rider* show the evolution of the biker lifestyle, from its humble beginnings as rebels without a cause finding the thrill of riding and racing motorcycles in *The Wild One*, to the Hells Angels–inspired plot of "Live to ride, ride to live" and screw authority practiced in *The Wild Angels*, to the more philosophical trappings found in *Easy Rider*.

All these lessons, whether total fiction, inspired by actual incidents and captured in film, or torn from the morning newspaper as gospel truth have become snapshots in our mass mind that have helped form our opinions of who bikers are. I believe that the modern concept of the outlaw biker sprang fully grown, fangs in place and dripping with blood, from a deep-seated primal fear that had the United States running scared at the end of World War II.

It is true that servicemen returned from war as very different cats than the fresh-faced boys who marched off to battle. As has

> We take our children, turn them into killing machines, send them to hell to murder people, then drag their asses back here to Disneyland and tell them to just go back to being the sweet kids they were before.

George Christie and the Olympic torch. Looks like he stepped right out of a David Mann painting.

been the case in every war since, people came home fucked up in the heads in a major way by the horrors of war. They experienced stuff that no human being should ever have to be put through, all because they were trying to be good Americans and do what Uncle Sam told them to, no matter how twisted. So men came home from war and rode motorcycles to blow off a little steam and they hung out with other vets who were into bikes because they were the only people on earth who understood the bullshit they went through.

So get this: We take our children, turn them into killing machines, send them to hell to murder people, then drag their asses back here to Disneyland and tell them to just go back to being the sweet kids they were before. Right. And here's the real capper: Do you know what Americans are more afraid of than anything, even more afraid of than losing their sacred collection of stuff? They're afraid that their children will turn into monsters. We're all scared to death that our little girls will turn into zombies and eat their mommies just like in *Night of the Living Dead*. We're all petrified that our little boys will pick up a butcher knife and become Michael Meyers in *Halloween*, slicing up the entire family into bite-size bits. That's what you call ironic.

THE UNDEAD

In fact, the reason that zombie movies have become so popular may have to do with the fact that we are all just a step away from becoming soulless, undead things that feed off the living. That's what consumers do, right? Maybe that's why George Romero had his zombies hang out at the mall in *Dawn of the Dead*, a place they had happy memories of, or maybe shopping is in our very DNA. The social commentary in zombie movies is clear, whether the reanimation of corpses is a mystery or a harbinger of the end days as in George Romero's films, or the undead are created by a plague virus in films like *I Am Legend, 28 Days*, or the five *Resident Evil* movies; it's obvious that we are the zombies. These films are telling us that the concept of manifest destiny is wrong and that you can't just keep expanding unchecked for eternity. Eventually, something is gonna pop, and that's where we find ourselves right now.

As mentioned in Chapter Two, the powers that be in America decided to ramp up the economy after World War II, creating a massive advertising campaign spewed into our brains nonstop by the media (radio, TV, and newspapers), and, sure enough, turned us all into zombies looking for a brighter smile and a smarter smart phone. As the police chief said in *Night of the Living Dead*, "You kill the brain, you kill the ghoul." Apparently, only killing the brain will stop the influx of advertising messages.

We define ourselves by the stuff we have, which in turn is determined by how much we earn, which is determined by what we do for a living. That's why the first thing people ask each other when they initially meet is "What do you do for a living?"

> The reason that zombie movies have become so popular may have to do with the fact that we are all just a step away from becoming soulless, undead things that feed off the living.

In the grand scheme of things, defining ourselves by what our jobs are and how much we earn is a relatively recent development. I don't mean that people just sat around on their asses—before we had jobs, as we now know them, people worked hard just to stay alive. They wove fabric and sewed clothing, they raised grain and milled the grain, they raised livestock and cared for (and butchered and ate) the livestock. To get what they didn't create themselves, they traded what they did create. The cobbler would trade shoes for flour and meat. The sheep herder would trade mutton and raw wool for cotton fabric and dairy products.

For the first 200,000-odd years that modern humans roamed the planet, this system worked pretty well. In fact, by the late Middle Ages, the population of Europe was thriving under such a system.

But one group wasn't thriving—the wealthy aristocracy. Rather than working, this group earned its income from extracting money from the workers in the form of taxes and other tributes. The aristocracy received its tithings simply because of who it was, its lineage, and its noble rank. As people became more proficient at providing for their needs, they became less impressed with the dipshits in the aristocracy and the tributes began to dry up.

Since the aristocracy really didn't have any skills or talents, producing its own shit wasn't really an option, so it figured out a way to gain control of the thriving barter-based economy. To accomplish this, it developed the chartered monopoly. In this system the state enacted laws that only allowed officially sanctioned corporations to engage in most forms of commerce, shutting down many of the independent businesspeople who had previously enjoyed a

```
No one owns a
one percenter's ass.
```

sustainable lifestyle by bartering the goods they produced for the goods other craftsmen and tradesmen produced and forcing them to get jobs with the officially sanctioned corporations.

People began to buy into this bullshit until they no longer questioned its truth. Now it is the way of the world. The corporations produce stuff for us to buy and we borrow money to buy their stuff, which in turn enslaves us to the corporations. The more stuff we buy, the less free we are to tell the corporations to go fuck themselves. In the end, the company store not only owns our souls, it owns our asses.

No one owns a one percenter's ass. The one percenter does not define himself by his job; he defines himself by his passion: his passion for motorcycles, his passion for freedom, his passion for life. In large part, this unwillingness to sell out to the corporate world is at the root of his battles with the rest of society.

FILLING YOUR HOLE

As decades have passed since the end of World War II, Americans have become fully entrenched in the idea that happiness is only found in the temporary thrill of buying and owning a whole bunch of stuff that you don't need and that will never fill the hole in your heart. Many one percenters have figured out that true happiness is not found in buying stuff, but rather in belonging to something and being about something that is grander than yourself. For those whose motorcycle club comes first in their lives, belonging to something takes away the need for the temporary fix that loading up on a bunch of crap provides. However, this "belonging to something" has

Bikers are among the most loyal and patriotic Americans you will ever meet.

its own track of evolution and we'll talk about that a bit later, but first, a few words about the American corrections system.

In a society that brainwashes its citizens into believing that we are about our stuff and not about each other, there is a system of checks and balances. The way it works is simple: Work hard and you can buy a lot of crap you don't need so you'll have the illusion that your life is fulfilled. However, step out of line in any way and society will send in the goon squad to arrest you and throw your ass in prison. The absolute worst thing they can do to consumers in this country is to throw them in prison because then they lose their jobs and all their stuff! They can't pay their bills when they're in prison, so they lose their houses and their cars and their flat-screen TVs. Horrors!

One of the flaws in this system is that some Americans, such as the one percenter, don't really give a shit where you house their bodies because you can't take away their freedom and you can't own their souls. The One Percenter Code reminds us that freedom lies inside each of us and can never be taken away.

PRI-ZEN

One of the byproducts of the RICO Act is that a lot of one percenter motorcycle club members have done prison time, or are doing prison time right now. While the One Percenter Code is still in effect among bikers behind the walls, there are some interesting variations on the theme. American prisons are composed of whites, blacks, Hispanics, and a very small percentage of others, such as Asians and Native Americans. The largest percentage of inmates held in most American prisons is black, followed by inmates who are Hispanic, followed by those who are white.

The prison inmate code mandates that you stay with your own racial group, no matter what. Take everything you know about society outside the walls and throw it away once they rack those bars

Step out of line in any way and society will send in the goon squad to arrest you and throw your ass in prison.

shut. On the inside, you hang with your own if you want to survive. For whites, you have a whole lot of people who are in for drugs and a whole lot of bikers who got snared by the RICO Act.

Bikers hang with other bikers in prison, and generally speaking, even if your club is at war with another club, prison is a neutral zone. You don't start shit with another one percenter on the inside because you will cause ripple effects out in the world and also because you need every down peckerwood in the joint to have your back if a race riot breaks out. If you're not about something in the Graybar Hotel, you find yourself alone and without backup, and you might just find yourself bleeding to death from being stabbed in the neck. Pleasant thought, eh?

The One Percenter Code on the inside tells you that you hang with your own, you talk about motorcycles, you share your issues of *Easyriders* magazine, and you dream of riding when you get out. You do your own time and learn to not let the time do you. You keep to your program and get through being down one day at a time.

There is a state of Zen in living each day one moment at a time, in a state of constant now, and prison can offer that if you choose to do your time that way. Think about it: If you make every *now* the best it can be (within your power), then you automatically have good memories of your past and you set yourself up for the best possible future. Make every *now* a perfect moment and the rest will take care of itself. Hell, whole books have been written about that and I just gave it to you in one paragraph.

SILENCE IS GOLDEN

The main thing for a one percenter to remember when on the inside is to keep his mouth shut and do his time. Some bikers in prison occasionally get the idea that they can better their situation, maybe even get less time, if they give someone up. This is called being a snitch (no, not the golden flying ball in the Harry Potter books and movies), and among one percenters a snitch is the lowest form of life on earth. If you want to get dead real quick in the pen, become a snitch. Talk about a ripple effect; not only can being a snitch get you killed, but it can start a major war between clubs on the outside.

Other rules in the One Percenter Code pertain to etiquette when your club is at war with another MC. Knowing that the other club may be showing up at public events, the president and officers may decide that all members will stop wearing their colors for a time. This is not done out of fear of the other MC, but with the knowledge that cops will be looking extra hard at your club until things blow over. It's best to lay low sometimes.

Another rule during club wartime is that you never bring heat to your house, another member's house, a member of the other club's house, or your job. The reasons for this are simple. First, because even in war, you have standards and principles, plus nobody wants the cops showin' up at their house or job. It will reflect badly on you and the club.

Even in club wars, there is respect for the other club's patch. They have earned the right to fly their colors, even if both clubs are sworn enemies. It's kinda like that old saying by Evelyn Beatrice Hall: "I disapprove of what you say, but I will defend to the death your right to say it." One percenters believe in the right to earn and wear your patch. They understand what club members had to go through to become patch holders.

Being a one percenter is more than a lifestyle; it is truly a way of life.

> If you want to get dead
> real quick in the pen,
> become a snitch.

There's another old saying in prison: "You can kill me, but you can't eat me." This has to do with the fact that though the legal system may lock the body away or even kill the body, it cannot chain the soul. You cannot have me if I choose not to let you. The real me that exists beyond this body is untouchable, so you can kill me but you will never *have* me. Veterans of war know this. Prisoners and slaves know this. Bikers know this.

BE SEEING YOU

I am often amazed by how fast things are changing in our world. It has been said that we will see more change in our lifetimes than has happened in the last hundred lifetimes of our ancestors. Everything just keeps speeding up, from communications and technology to our evolution as spiritual beings. I'm also amazed to be living in a tiny window in time in which we have internal combustion engines that are used to transport us in cars and on motorcycles. I mean, motorcycles only came about a little more than 100 years ago, and 50 years from now, whatever we'll be riding will be powered by something other than gasoline. Maybe we'll be riding electric bikes, such as the ones produced by Brammo in Ashland, Oregon. Their Enertia and Empulse electric motorcycles can travel up to 100 miles per hour and have a range of 60 miles.

As the editor of *Easyriders* magazine, I'm often asked what the future might hold for motorcycles, especially custom motorcycles like choppers. I tell people that it ultimately doesn't matter what power source drives the vehicles of the future. For as long as there have been automobiles and motorcycles, there have been people who just

> We will see more change
> in our lifetimes than has
> happened in the last hundred
> lifetimes of our ancestors.

have to cut them up, lower them, and custom paint them. We may be riding electric choppers or hydrogen-powered baggers someday, but I guarantee you that someone will chop them, make them look cool, and throw a flame paint job on 'em—and we'll be there!

Did you know that the world's very last typewriter factory went out of business recently? Yep, gone the way of the mimeograph machine, the eight-track tape deck, and the two-bit blow job. Godrej & Boyce in Mumbai, India, the very last company on earth still building typewriters, closed its doors at the end of April 2011. In a world of computers and Internet communication, who types letters? What else is coming to the extinction pile near you in our lifetime?

How about check writing? Europe is ahead of us on this already. Great Britain hopes to do away with paper checks by 2018 since it costs financial systems billions of dollars each year to process checks. Plastic debit cards, credit cards, and online banking will make check writing a thing of the past; plus, with online banking, it's easier to balance your accounts. And this leads us to . . .

The U.S. Postal Service will someday go the way of the dodo bird, and sooner rather than later, the way things are going. What do you get from your mailman? You get junk mail and bills. Everything else comes to your house by e-mail, UPS, or FedEx. So if you're getting all your billing online and paying them online, how can the post office stay in business? It is already pricing itself out of existence and UPS is often faster. Handwritten letters are also on the decline. Worldwide, approximately 183 billion e-mails are sent each day; that's two million each second. By November 2007, an estimated 3.3 billion people owned cell phones, and 80 percent of the world's population had access to cell phone coverage. Imagine how many text messages blast through the Noosphere every second! So long, mailman.

Newspapers are becoming extinct because baby boomers are the last generation still attached to getting news this way. Younger readers generally don't read or subscribe to newspapers because they would rather get their information instantly on the Internet or on cable TV news. Publishers have had to switch over to online subscriptions to make a buck, and the jury is still out on whether or not anyone will bother to pay for what they can get free on the Web. Likewise, the Yellow Pages will go the way of the milkman soon enough. Online search engines are getting more and more sophisticated, offering instant access and even dialing your phone for you. Research suggests that producing newspapers and print versions of the Yellow Pages will fall off 10 percent this year.

Printed classified ads will soon vanish thanks to the use of Craiglist and eBay to shop, buy, and sell stuff. And speaking of the Internet, dial-up Web access will soon be a thing of the past. Dial-up connections have fallen from 40 percent in 2001 to 10 percent in 2008. The combination of an infrastructure to accommodate affordable high-speed Internet connections and the disappearing home phone has all but killed dial-up access. According to a survey from the National Center for Health Statistics, at the end of 2007, nearly one in six homes was cell phone only, and, of those homes that had landlines, one in eight only received calls on their cells.

Have you noticed all the video rental stores disappearing? Why drive to the store to rent a DVD when you can pull up Netflix or On Demand and get the movie you want right now for less money? Unfortunately, this means a lot of the cool mom-and-pop stores that had all those hard-to-find movies like *Werewolves on Wheels* are out of biz too. Since we're talking about DVDs, when was the last time you pulled out a VHS videotape to watch it? With the ability to burn your own DVD right from your computer, collecting home movies on tape is dead, dead, dead.

Incandescent light bulbs are disappearing faster than the bluefin tuna. Before a few years ago, the standard 60-watt bulb was the mainstay of every U.S. home. Now, compact fluorescent light bulbs are largely replacing the older, Edison-era bulbs, which will be all but extinct within this decade.

Some say that books are going away, though I sincerely hope not. Online bookstores, such as Amazon, feature downloadable reading material for your digital notebook for less cost than buying a printed version. This is already affecting the number of bookstores from coast to coast. I am a member of the generation that still cherishes books and printed magazines, but this could all change in one generation or two.

Besides changing the way we rent movies and read, digital entertainment also changes the way you buy music. Soon, everything will exist virtually and you won't need to own a collection of music CDs or DVD movies, or even printed books because everything will always be available in the great oracle known as the Internet. However, I suggest you learn to play the guitar in case the power goes out. With all this change and technological sophistication, the most frightening thing to me about the new world we live in is the fact that our freedoms as individuals are disappearing. I was a big fan of the 1967 TV series *The Prisoner* starring Patrick McGoohan because of its "big brother is always watching" theme and the idea that the rights of the individual is all an illusion.

The series' concept that our names are replaced by numbers (McGoohan was designated as 6) seems very innocent today, when we are only known by numbers, from our banking accounts to our police records, from our driver's licenses to our various online profiles. McGoohan's imagined future world included video cameras everywhere and a total lack of privacy. In a time where our homes are constantly watched over by Google Earth and we can be located by GPS every minute of every day, it looks like his

The most frightening thing to me about the new world we live in is the fact that our freedoms as individuals are disappearing.

You can live your life proudly, do the right thing, and be about something, or you can be scared of everything and be about nothing. It's your choice.

nightmare has come true. As the brainwashed citizens of *The Prisoner*, who were always under surveillance in the village, often saluted, "Be seeing you."

THE GREAT SPEEDUP

Technology isn't the only thing moving at warp speed; according to a recent article by *Mother Jones* magazine, so are you! In "All Work and No Pay: The Great Speedup," Monika Bauerlein and Clara Jeffery state that workers in America are constantly being asked to do a whole lot more work for the same or less pay. From bus drivers, hospital technicians, construction workers, doctors, and lawyers, to professionals in such creative outlets as journalism and the film industry, employees are feeling that no matter how hard they try to keep up with working extra hours and taking on extra tasks, they are, in fact, falling behind.

Webster's Dictionary defines *speedup* as "an employer's demand for accelerated output without increased pay." This began in factories when employers would speed up the production line to fill big orders. According to the article, American blue-collar and

> In a world gone soft, the
> time has come to go outlaw!

white-collar workers no longer even acknowledge when extra tasks are asked of them. The extra work falls under the term "productivity," the implication being that if you don't pull your weight, you'll be fired. While this might be good for business, it's not good for workers who are expected to do more and more until they fail. We aren't working smarter, just harder, as productivity surges but wages have stagnated. According to "The Great Speedup," if the median household income had kept pace with the economy since 1970, it would now be nearly $92,000, not $50,000.

Americans now put in an average of 122 more hours at work per year than British workers and 378 more hours than German workers. Hey, no one wants to be called a slacker, but this is ridiculous.

Other than U.S. jobs going overseas and laid-off workers not getting rehired, there is also what is called offloading, which cuts jobs and dumps more work on remaining staff. A recent *Wall Street Journal* story discovered that more than half of the workers surveyed said their jobs had expanded without a raise in pay.

According to a report by the Economic Policy Institute, while U.S. productivity increased twice as fast in 2009 as it did in 2008, and twice as fast again in 2010, the number of workers was down and corporate profits were up 22 percent since 2007. These money-grubbing companies are pulling the wool over their employees' eyes and it's working! In fact, employees who manage to hold onto their jobs these days imagine that they are damned lucky to still have a job and put up with doing whatever the employer wants of them. We're right back to the fear of losing our precious stuff. Working citizens in this country are petrified that they will either be passed over or downsized, or just become obsolete. It all amounts to the same thing: If you lose your job, you'll lose your stuff.

The unemployment rate is twice as high among college graduates today as it was in 2007, and that's not counting people with bachelor's degrees who are waiting tables or stocking shelves. For those Americans who still have a job, a staggering 90 percent have watched their incomes dwindle for the past 30 years!

How did this happen? It happened because Americans wimped out! We got here thanks to decades of bad political decisions—turning over the financing of elections to the wealthy, making it impossible for unions to organize, and cutting the balls off of those whose job it was to regulate the greed heads on Wall Street.

Speaking of testicles, the American people need to grow a collective set, big meaty ones, and take back this country. The One Percenter Code demands that you stand up for what you believe in. In a world gone soft, the time has come to go outlaw! America has learned the hard way that "You've got to stand for something or you'll fall for anything."

GOD FORGIVES; ONE PERCENTERS DON'T... OR AT LEAST THEY DIDN'T . . .

While the image of the one percenter conjures up visions of axe-wielding Vikings, Huns on war ponies, or Conan on a Harley, motorcycle clubs have learned to work within the system to effect change. Believe it or not, there are patch holder lawyers and even ministers. MCs have learned to use their collective brain over brawn to overcome trumped-up charges against them more times than you would believe. One percenters have had to become the iron fist in a velvet glove in order to fight and win in today's world.

As technology and society continue to change and evolve, so do one percenters and so does the code they live by. It's not unusual to see one percenter motorcycle clubs engaged in their local community these days, participating in charity runs and events, and giving back to their town. There have been many stories of motorcycle clubs opening up clubhouses in the worst part of town, where shootings, drug dealing, and prostitution is running rampant, only to clean those neighborhoods up for the community. Yep, even wolves take care of their cubs and clean up the streets.

In the end, it's all about brotherhood.

Bikers have families too. They go to Disneyland, they go to church, they drive their kids to soccer practice, and they pass along their way of life to their kids. In recent years, changes in society have caused changes within the one percenter community as well. Hardcore bikers who had no place in their hearts for forgiveness 20 years ago are realizing that they must include such ideals if they are to leave something meaningful behind for their children and their children's children. It has given "being about something" a whole new meaning.

Many spiritual teachings stress the importance of forgiveness. The book and study series called *A Course in Miracles* explains forgiveness as the following: "Recognizing that what you thought your brother did to you has not occurred. It does not pardon the sins and make them real; rather it sees that there was no sin in the first place, and therefore, all sins are forgiven."

But true forgiveness is really all about taking responsibility for your life experiences. Bikers know this is true. People who annoy us, make us angry, or even inspire hatred are actually just symbolic aspects of what we need to forgive about ourselves. Often, this concept is hard won and difficult to swallow.

We project our need for forgiveness outward, but the only way to be free of this pattern of thought (because that is all it is) is to forgive your own dark side as seen in others you meet. How do you do this? You change your mind. It is actually that simple. Change your mind about your projected image of others and what you imagine they have done to you to evoke your wrath. Imagine such people as illusions in a dream (because that is what all this really is, ya know). When you do this, and see everyone you encounter as innocent and helpful spirits who are here to help you learn on your path toward enlightenment, the illusion you have created, based in fear, will dissolve. Didn't think you'd be getting a crash course in spirituality in a book about outlaw bikers, did you?

Okay, I can hear you out there. Several of you just yelled, "Bullshit!" The bottom line is this: No one can take away your tranquility and inner peace unless you decide to give it away to them. You decide. Moment by moment, we each create the reality we decide to be in and we can make every experience good, bad, or indifferent. I've seen this concept put into practice inside motorcycle clubs. Believe it or not, I've seen the president of a club pull everyone back from a quick, knee-jerk reaction to some perceived wrong or disrespect done to a patch holder or the club. I've seen cooler minds prevail. If one percenters were the brutes that the media has programmed us to believe them to be, there would be blood in the streets. Instead, more often than not, there is peace.

BAFFLE THEM WITH BULLSHIT

By the same token, the media-induced concept that has been enforced by the police and the ATF, and even the FBI, is that one percenter motorcycle clubs are notorious crime syndicates that control worldwide drug trafficking, gun running, and prostitution. This is utterly ridiculous poppycock. I'm not saying that individual

> One percenters throw down the bloody gauntlet of rebellion and bellow, "None but men of valor shall pass."

members of motorcycle clubs haven't ever sold an illegal gun or some drugs, but so have individual members of the Moose Lodge or the Elks, or the guy in your town who drives the ice cream truck. The problem with the RICO Act is that if one member of a club does something illegal, the whole club can go down for it. Now, knowing this, if you were a member of a one percenter MC, wouldn't you make damned sure your patch holders are clean? Wouldn't you go out of your way to steer clear of the po po?

Traditionally, one percenters have been portrayed as being wrapped up in dreary little egos that demand respect; they have been seen as Neanderthals and bullies. But when you are tied up in a belief system that refuses to forgive, you enter a world of hurt. It is a system that doesn't work for anybody—least of all you, if that's your frame of mind.

As one percenters eventually get married, have babies, raise families, become grandfathers, and finally see their own mortality staring them in the face, a shift occurs. Some of that big bad biker ego drops away as they realize that nothing in this temporal world is real or lasts. No matter what you accomplish in this lifetime, eventually you realize that none of it really matters. Being here is not about making money, or having a lot of sex, drugs, and rock 'n' roll . . . . Sorry to disappoint you.

We live in a time of instant gratification, when anything we desire can be had for a price, right now. But no matter how many cool things you buy, or how many cool motorcycles you ride, or how many chicks you sleep with, there will always be that hole in your gut that tells you something is missing. That's because this world is an illusion.

Eventually, seasoned one percenters who have spent their lives raging at the machine and flipping the world the finger mellow out a bit. You don't ride with the reaper perched on your shoulder for a lifetime without learning a thing or two about life, death, and the big picture. You learn not to sweat the petty things.

The biker lifestyle has indeed evolved over time and the One Percenter Code has grown and adjusted itself to meet the needs of the times. This code of conduct was perhaps born on the battlefield, was tested and tried, was forged to make hearts of steel. It has since known the prejudice of closed minds and limited beliefs. Bikers have become what they have needed to be in order to survive in a world with little use for them. Society has a problem with one percenters because they don't fit into the convenient mold of complacency devised by our forefathers in order to create a civilization that is both civil and obedient. Rebels fight this sort of thing tooth and nail, and the One Percenter Code is carved in the living rock of ages to stand for the individual.

Just as did knights of old, one percenters throw down the bloody gauntlet of rebellion and bellow, "None but men of valor shall pass." It is a call that is as old as humanity itself and in its creed there are more than rules and regulations; there is the realization that as human beings, perhaps we are something more than we appear on the surface. In all cultures, in all lands and times, men have gazed up into the night sky filled with stars and asked the big questions: Who am I? Why am I here? What is the meaning of life? At some point all men and women look within to try to discover the source of their heartache and despair.

Bikers occasionally figure out that something is missing in their lives just as we all do. And that, my friends, is when one percenters realize who they really are. For we are all part of the source, we are all part of God. Every single person who is put in your path in life, for apparent good or ill, is in service to God and is an aspect of divine order. Each is in your world for a reason and has a gift of learning to give you. It's up to you whether or not you choose to watch, listen, and learn from it.

So the One Percenter Code is passed on from generation to generation, offering a way of life and a moral center upon which to build a life.

7.
REBEL
SCHOOL

HOW GRAYBEARDS
PASS THE BIKER WAY OF LIFE
ON TO A NEW GENERATION
OF RIDERS

> "We must be willing to get rid of the life we've planned, so as to have the life that is waiting for us."
>
> —Joseph Campbell

Do you know how this book project began? It began with a need that Darwin Holmstrom, my editor at Motorbooks, and I feel must be filled in this world. Namely, that there is no guidebook on how to be a man in our society today. There is no book of rules and regulations or codes of conduct for boys to take to heart in order to become a well-rounded, decent male human being.

So Darwin and I set out to create such a guidebook. I remember he said to me, "How does a boy become a real man today in a world gone soft?" That's how *One Percenter Code* was born. After about a year of deliberation and study, interviewing members of one percenter motorcycle clubs, reading everything ever written on the subject, and comprising a lifetime of personal stories and experiences, we put together the book you are holding. *One Percenter Code: How to Be an Outlaw in a World Gone Soft* should begin where *One Percenter: Legend of the Outlaw Biker* left off, Darwin told me. And here we are.

Up until now the only way to learn the One Percenter Code was to be taught by another one percenter. This code of conduct and way of life has been passed down verbally, through experience and action directly, father to son, or grandfather to grandson, or brother to brother since the 1940s. As mentioned earlier, many of these teachings come from moral creeds and spiritual practices that go back thousands of years. But the One Percenter Code has much in common with both the Code of the West and the older Code of Chivalry practiced by knights. Both of these codes focus on courtesy, compassion, and courage.

A Code of Chivalry was documented in *The Song of Roland* in the Middle Ages during the rule of William the Conqueror (1066) and is known as Charlemagne's Code of Chivalry. *The Song of Roland* was composed between 1098 and 1100, describing the betrayal of Count Roland by Ganelon and his resulting death in the Pyranee Mountains at the hands of the Saracens. Roland was a loyal defender of Lord Charlemagne and his Code of Chivalry includes the following:

The Urban Dictionary defines brotherhood as "a group of close friends who will do anything for each other no matter what time of day or night it is."

The one percenter code of conduct and way of life has been passed down verbally, through experience and action directly, father to son, or grandfather to grandson, or brother to brother since the 1940s.

- To fear God and maintain his church
- To serve the liege lord in valor and faith
- To protect the weak and defenseless
- To give succor to widows and orphans
- To refrain from the wanton giving of offense
- To live by honor and for glory
- To despise pecuniary reward
- To fight for the welfare of all
- To guard the honor of fellow knights
- To eschew unfairness, meanness, and deceit
- To keep faith
- To speak the truth at all times
- To persevere to the end in any enterprise begun
- To respect the honor of women
- To never refuse a challenge from an equal
- To never turn your back on a foe (generally good advice)

Notice how many of the previous points are synonymous with those found in the Code of the West? *To serve the liege lord* becomes "lay down your life for your outfit." *To respect the honor of women* becomes "treat women like ladies." *At all times speak the truth* becomes "your word is your bond." *Live each day with courage* becomes "live each day with courage." You get the idea.

When a boy listens to tales read by his father or grandfather of knights of old, or pirates, or cowboys, no doubt some of the moral

> Boys look up to the adult men in their life, and in the world of the outlaw biker, kids grow up around club members and look up to patch holders.

lessons learned in these stories stick. Boys look up to the adult men in their life, and in the world of the outlaw biker, kids grow up around club members and look up to patch holders as if they are knights on iron steeds, for bikers are larger-than-life characters. To a child, one percenters embody many of the noble assets of storybook knights, pirates, and cowboys. All are mythic characters, reluctant heroes who do battle in various arenas.

TOUGH LOVE

What many of today's parents might think of as tough love amounts to just another day for a boy growing up around one percenters. For instance, I have a friend who is a one percenter in southern California and owns a car repair shop. He has a teenage son who works in the shop after school to learn the valuable lessons of how to wrench on vehicles and deal with all sorts of customers. One day I stopped by after hours, and the dad and son were working together on building a custom bike that will be the boy's first motorcycle. That's what people today call "male bonding."

Anyway, the dad was wrenchin' away and the kid had wandered off into the office where he had one of those cool, life-draining devices known as a PlayStation 3. The kid was blowing away aliens to his heart's content while his father was toiling on the bike that will someday belong to the kid. When I was a teen, if my dad and I had been building me a motorcycle, you can bet your ass that I would have been right there beside him until the cows came home,

The One Percenter Code is passed on from brother to brother and passed down from grandfather to father to son.

learning as much as I could about how to build a bike. Not so for this one percenter's son.

My friend called out to his kid several times, needing his help to position and install the Springer front end, but the sound of the PS3 was blasting away as the kid rocked out killing alien critters. Finally, the dad heaved a sigh, walked out of the shop and into the office, quietly took the game controller from his kid's hands and walked out of the office. I'll never forget how the teenager's mouth hung open in a weird mixture of shock, bewilderment, and a tinge of fear. He slowly walked out into the shop to see his father place the controller in a vice. The dad tightened it in place, whistling a happy tune, then picked up a big mallet and smashed the controller to smithereens!

> The dad tightened the video-game controller in the vice, whistling a happy tune, then picked up a big mallet and smashed the controller to smithereens!

The one percenter released the remains of the device from the vice and handed them back to the boy saying, "Now, I could use a little help with your bike." You can bet that kid was very attentive to helping build his motorcycle after that.

COURTESY

You can tell a lot about how a man was raised by the simplest things. Courtesy is one of those attributes that is mighty rare these days. I was in D&S Harley-Davidson in Phoenix, Oregon, recently, sitting at a table and sipping coffee as I waited to pick up my 1966 FLH from service. The couch and chairs in the waiting room were fairly full of patrons. A young guy in his early 20s walked up and looked around for a place to sit, then, seeing me sitting alone at the table with three open chairs, sauntered over and asked politely if he could join me. I waved my hand at an open chair and invited him to sit down. This guy had a proper upbringing.

I continued reading the local newspaper and the young guy took out a journal and started writing notes. I figured he was a college kid, working on a paper, but it was nice to see the notebook instead of a laptop (call me old-fashioned).

About 10 minutes later an old coot in his late 60s or early 70s waddled over and just sat his ass down on one of the remaining chairs without a "good morning" or a "kiss my ass." See, the thing about old-timers is they have earned the right to be crotchety and not give a shit, so I didn't take offense, but if he had been a dude in his 40s, his disregard for common courtesy would have pissed me off.

The look of a chopper with a small front tire, which imitated the look of a car set up for drag racing, was popular for a brief time in the 1970s, at least until riders realized that the radically altered frames on choppers of the period required the stability of a 21-inch front hoop.

I grew up in the South, North Carolina, to be exact. Now down there, you are always polite to folks and you respect your elders. You also *always* speak to someone. You make sure to offer up a cheery, "Good mornin'" to every living soul you come across. And God strike down the infidel who doesn't return a greeting. In the South, if an arrogant asshole doesn't give you a howdy back, you have the perfect right to slap the taste outta his Yankee mouth. Sorry, I got carried away there.

The point is, as John Gilbert said, "You can always tell a guy who hasn't had his beating." Courtesy is a cornerstone of proper social conduct. You can bet that you sure as hell better be courteous around one percenters because they don't take shit from anybody.

> In the South, if an arrogant asshole doesn't give you a howdy back, you have the perfect right to slap the taste outta his Yankee mouth.

One percenter courtesy extends beyond just saying "howdy," "please," and "thank you." One percenters give more to their communities than just about any other group; believe it or not, there are few groups or organizations in this country that bring in more dollars to charities than bikers.

COMPASSION

Just as I mentioned forgiveness in the last chapter, compassion is a trait that one would not normally associate with one percenters, yet there is evidence of it all around you. The country's most notorious one percenter motorcycle clubs actively participate in charity runs, rallies, and events that extend to major cities all across America. You'll find that bikers have a soft spot when it comes to kids and animals; they show great compassion both as a group and individually when it comes to giving back to their community. One percenter motorcycle clubs lend a helping hand to animal shelters, wildlife preserves, children's hospitals, juveniles with diabetes, reading and educational programs, and blood drives, and some motorcycle clubs have even set aside time and money to create playgrounds for disadvantaged kids.

Compassion is often a byproduct of age, and when a one percenter has a family, produces children and then grandchildren, his heart goes out to those in need. This is in keeping with the knight's Code of Chivalry and the Code of the West, which both teach kindness to the weak and those in distress.

When speaking of compassion, there is no greater source of knowledge than the Dalai Lama. His Holiness often speaks on this universal subject and has said the following:

> To experience genuine compassion is to develop a feeling of closeness to others combined with a sense of responsibility for their welfare. True compassion develops when we ourselves want happiness and not suffering for others, and recognize that they have every right to pursue this.
>
> Compassion compels us to reach out to all living beings, including our so-called enemies, those people who upset or hurt us. Irrespective of what they do to you, if you remember that all beings like you are only trying to be happy, you will find it much easier to develop compassion towards them. Usually your sense of compassion is limited and biased. We extend such feelings only towards our family and friends or those who are helpful to us. People we perceive as enemies and others to whom we are indifferent are excluded from our concern. That is not genuine compassion. True compassion is universal in scope. It is accompanied by a feeling of responsibility. To act altruistically, concerned only for the welfare of others, with no selfish or ulterior motives, is to affirm a sense of universal responsibility.

COURAGE

In the Middle Ages, bravery or courage was referred to as fortitude, that ability to hang in there in the most dire of situations. As Winston Churchill was quoted as saying, "Courage is rightly esteemed the first of human qualities because it is the quality that guarantees all others."

Ernest Hemingway defined courage as grace under pressure. In our modern world, we often think of courage as the ability to stand up for what you believe in, even if by so doing, your actions might result in social disapproval, injury, or even death. Courage is basically putting your life on the line for what you believe in.

Bikers know that every time they throw a leg over their motorcycle and start it up to go for a ride that it might be their last.

A jockey shift—that is, a shifter that has been
modified to be hand shifted rather than foot
shifted—is also known as a "suicide shift," mostly
because the ill-handling chopper to which it's
usually attached is normally trying to kill its
rider even when he has both hands on the handlebar.

We all roll with the Grim Reaper at our shoulder, aware that the
slightest miscalculation or a bit of gravel on the road could cause a
life-threatening spill. Even though we know this, we still ride our
motorcycles. We don't think of it as courage; it's just that we live to
ride. . . . What else would we do? And when we fall off our bikes,
we get up and get right back on.

Members of one percenter motorcycle clubs put their lives on the
line for their club every time they fly their colors. One percenters
have their brothers' backs no matter what and that takes a special
type of courage. One percenters will take a bullet for their club and
stand up tall and proud no matter what.

> Bikers know that every time
> they throw a leg over their
> motorcycle and start it up
> to go for a ride that it
> might be their last.

Bikers have the kind of heart that keeps them from stepping down when most people would be running their asses away from a situation. I remember reporting on a biker who saw a hit-and-run accident. He twisted the throttle on his Harley and chased the car down, taking his life in his hands for a complete stranger. He came up alongside the car and kicked the driver's door in. The driver went off the road and came to a halt, then the biker dragged his ass out of the car and held him for the police. When the camera crews eventually caught up with him, the biker just shrugged his shoulders and said, "That's what bikers do. I didn't think about the fact that I was putting myself in harm's way. I just went after that dude. It was the right thing to do." That's courage.

EFFED IN THE A

If you're feeling a little fucked right now, join the club. Our entire society is effed in the A these days, so you're not alone. Five years ago, most of us had job security. We had problems, but it looked like we would all have jobs for the foreseeable future. The most stressful thing for people who had been working at the same job for many years was wondering whether or not they would ever get another promotion. The concept of losing our jobs was inconceivable. Now one in five of us can't find work and those of us who have jobs could lose them at any minute. That kind of stress is untenable.

But really, what we fear is losing our stuff. We fear not being able to make our payments and going bankrupt so that we can't buy

> The one percenter would focus on what really matters. Like his club. Like his family.

more stuff. In other words, we fear failing the cocksuckers who have enslaved us by selling us all that needless stuff on credit.

Well, take a lesson from the one percenter. The one percenter would say, "Fuck those cocksuckers. Fuck them and all that stuff they want to sell us." The one percenter would focus on what really matters. Like his club. Like his family.

Take, as an example, the sales director at a marital-aid and sexual novelty device manufacturing company, who had planned to go on a weeklong motorcycle trip with his 80-year-old father, but then he had to prepare for yet another in a seemingly endless series of board meetings, so he trimmed the vacation down to two days. Then he canceled it altogether to prepare for this board meeting, so instead of hitting the road with his father, he spent the week creating spreadsheets explaining why the sales of butt plugs were declining in comparison to the sales of double-headed dildos. Thing is, no matter how hard he prepared, the evil cocksuckers who comprise the board were going to crucify him like they always did.

What he should have done was tell the evil cocksuckers to fuck themselves, phoned in his preparation for the board meeting, and gone on the trip with his father. He has the rest of his life to suck the rectal eye of evil cocksuckers on some board of directors or another, but he has a finite amount of time to take a motorcycle trip with his father. It really wasn't that hard a decision.

PASSING IT DOWN

As the editor of *Easyriders* magazine, I know a lot of bikers from all over the country, heck, from all over the world. And I know a lot of

The happiest people on earth are bikers
because they live in the moment and don't
worry about tomorrow.

bikers who are second- or third-generation riders. If your parents are bikers and you grow up in a biker household, one of two things usually happens: You either wind up as a biker yourself, or the values you learn keep you in good stead for a well-balanced and prosperous life. Case in point, I know a guy named Cary Brobeck who was raised in a one percenter household and now is in his late 30s. Cary still eats, sleeps, and breathes motorcycles. Riding is truly his life, yet he manages to balance his love for bikes with a good job and an awesome family. He's a responsible citizen, a hard worker, and a great husband and dad. I asked him to sum up some of the aspects of the One Percenter Code that were passed down to him from his father and that make him the man he is today. You will no doubt find that some of Cary's thoughts on the matter are very similar to the rules of biker etiquette found in the last chapter. Here's what he had to say:

> With all the pussification going on with today's youth, it amazes
> me that there are still a handful of guys who can kick start a

motorcycle. Along with losing touch with their manhood, today's kids have also lost touch with what it is, and what it was, to be a biker. There are some things in the biker world that may not be known to the common Joe Schmo or weekend warrior. Some biker etiquette, morals, and values need to be learned, passed down, if you will. Not everybody who rides has a one percenter dad or brother to pass this priceless information on to them. If you don't, think of this book as being that dad or brother you always wished you had.

The first and most important lesson to be learned is *respect*. Like most people, treat a biker with respect and you will get respect back. Act like a douche bag, and guess what? You'll probably end up getting a good thumpin'. There is no reason to run and cower because some patch holders from the local chapter of some MC walks into the bar. If you are on a bike or part of a riding club, go on over (at the appropriate time) and introduce yourself, maybe even buy them a beer. If you are not a "biker" or on a bike, just leave them alone. Trust me; they could not care less about the average guy in some random bar. You do, however, need to respect more than the one percenter himself. Respect their privacy, respect their colors, respect their

"I'd rather be riding my motorcycle and thinking about God than sitting in church thinking about my motorcycle."

bikes, and definitely respect their women. Basically respect everything they do if you want to be anywhere near the one percenter biker.

Brotherhood is another thing that I fear is going away with the skinny jean generation. Any one percenter will pretty much drop what he is doing or get up in the middle of the night to help out a brother. This value desperately needs to be passed down from generation to generation. I feel that our society has become a very selfish, "me-first" type of society. If more of the average Joes out there had a sense of brotherhood like one percenters do, this world would be a much better place. If your buddy calls you and asks for a hand, put down your smart phone and go help him out. Also, if you see a fellow biker broken down on the side of the road, pull over and see if you can help; it could be *you* who's broken down next time.

So far we have *respect* and *brotherhood*, the two most important biker values that can be passed down to the youngsters out there. Some of the other stuff that is a must-know for today's youth are [the concepts of] *hard work* and *dedication*. It seems as though kids these days want to start at the top. Whatever happened to setting a goal and working your ass off to achieve that goal? Ask any former hang-around or prospect how hard they had to work to get that patch on their back. That shit is earned, not given out to some whiney spoiled kid who wants to be a bad ass. If you put in half as much hard work as a prospect does to get his center patch, you will probably be very successful in whatever you do in life.

This brings us to *dedication*. About the only other organization I can think of that has the kind of dedication a one percenter motorcycle club demonstrates is the good ol' U.S. Armed Forces, and they are forced to have dedication. The one percenter chooses to have absolute dedication to his club. Go ahead and mock a club in front of a member if you want to find out just how dedicated they are. They will risk anything to defend a fellow brother or the integrity of the club, even if it means a little jail time for whoopin' some ass. You should have dedication in whatever you attempt in life, or failure is certain to happen. Whether you're dealing with your family, your job, or your motorcycle club, they all take dedication in order to work. It's easy to walk away, but a real man finishes what he starts.

More than good character needs to be passed on. There are also skills that should be passed on too. Not many youngsters can afford to go out and buy the newest Harley-Davidson Dyna or Street Glide. Most of today's youth are rollin' around on old Ironhead Sportsters. Old bikes have a lot of heart and soul if you ask me. But they also have lots of miles and wear and tear. A Harley manual can only get these kids so far. Someone needs to teach 'em that you can gap points with a business card or a cigarette box top. Someone needs to teach 'em to pull their sparkplugs and burn them with a lighter to clean them up a bit. Someone needs to teach them that when their gas cap flies off on the freeway you can use a condom over the hole to get you home . . . and so on.

THE MOTORCYCLE BOND

Nothing can bond a father and son together like the shared love of motorcycles. Automobiles often offer a similar bond since boys love to learn to wrench on anything with wheels and it's the father's job to teach his boy how to handle basic maintenance and how to drive or ride.

I asked a group of more than 50 bikers across the country to share stories about advice that was handed down to them from their fathers about taking care of their beloved scooters. Interestingly, many of the stories we heard boiled down to the following lessons that have been taught again and again to bikers everywhere. I know you'll hear familiar advice in these stories. Reading between the lines offers insights into more than wrenchin' and ridin', as true life lessons frequently sneak into the garage.

While a father might tell his son to stay in school and "make something of yourself," the basic lesson is that you never stop learning in this life. Whether you are learning to strip down an Evo motor, learning how to custom paint your bike, or are just encouraged to learn as much about motorcycles as you can, many bikers cite their fathers as the inspiration behind their enduring passion for two wheels.

> Nothing can bond a father and son together like the shared love of motorcycles.

"I remember trying to put a transmission back together," says Chris of Jacksonville, Florida. "Man, I had that thing all to pieces and I found out that taking it apart was a whole lot easier than putting it all back together. My dad taught me how to mark, label, and catalog all the parts, laying them out on a piece of butcher paper on the shop table so that I wouldn't have any extra parts sittin' around when I was done. Basically, he taught me to never give up, no matter what. 'You can fix it!' He would tell me. I'll always be thankful for the life lessons he gave me. Plus he had a real positive way to look at life. He was always making lemonade out of the lemons that life handed him."

"Pop told me to live in the now," Stan from Thousand Oaks, California, says. "He said that the happiest people on earth are bikers because we live in the moment and don't worry about tomorrow. He was the happiest man I ever met. He once told me, 'Only bikers know why dogs stick their heads out of car windows.'"

"Hey, shit happens! That's what my dad taught me," says Dennis from Kinston, North Carolina. "He said that life ain't fair and sometimes the assholes win. But he said it's what you do with the cards that are dealt to you that determines who you are. He also told me that nobody really knows who they are until they deal with a little pain."

"My father was a rancher and a biker, so he had the Code of the West thing down," says Billy from Provo, Utah. "He told me that sometimes even when you try your best, you still might fail. He said that 'the important thing in life is to live honestly, to always do the right thing and to never give up.' That's what I live by."

"My ol' man always told me that I was capable of doing anything if I set my mind to it," recalls Jim from Stroudsburg, Pennsylvania.

> "My ol' man always told me that I was capable of doing anything if I set my mind to it," recalls Jim from Stroudsburg, Pennsylvania.

"He would tell me, 'It's all up to you. You can make each day a great day or a lousy day depending on your attitude.' My dad is gone now, but I think of what he said to me every day."

"When in doubt, knock 'em out!" says Will from Louisville, Kentucky. "Dad was old-school and taught me never to put up with bullies in life. He told me that when it looked like I was gonna be in a fight, to be the first one to settle it by jumpin' in feet first and deckin' the motherfucker. He told me, 'Get in first and get out first.' He also said that people who walk around with chips on their shoulders often mistake kindness for weakness and you have to teach them the error of their ways."

"You talk about the ultimate optimist, that was my father," recalls Big Bill from Ventura, California. "He always said, 'Don't sweat the small stuff and it's *all* small stuff.' He said that folks either see the glass as half empty or half full but that he knew the glass had been all the way full, 'cause he just drank the top half!"

"I learned not to take life so seriously," says Paul from Kalamazoo, Michigan. "My dad rode his whole life and he told me, 'Do what you love and you'll never work a day in your life.' We shared a love of motorcycles and now I own a bike shop. He was right and now I tell my boys, 'Do what you love.' It's just good advice."

"Talk about a crazy ol' philosopher," Chuck from Atlanta, Georgia, told me. "My dad has a million sayings about riding. For instance, he says, 'I'd rather be riding my motorcycle and thinking about God than sitting in church thinking about my motorcycle.' He also says, 'Ever notice you never see a motorcycle parked in front of a psychiatrist's office?'"

"Ever notice that you never see a motorcycle parked
in front of a psychiatrist's office?"

"Never be afraid to try new things," says Jay from Rapid City, South Dakota. "I never knew my father, but my grandfather offered a lot of sage advice. He told me that life was too short to worry about anything and to try new things and learn new things every day."

"My dad actually told me that people are like motorcycles and you have to respect them if you want them to work for you," says Arne of Seattle, Washington. "He also told me that if I wanted people to respect me, I would have to respect them first."

"Never bring a knife to a gun fight," says Hooper from Dallas, Texas. "My pop has a great sense of humor, but he is like a pitbull in a fight. I would never want to cross him. Right now he is seventy-eight years old and I still respect the shit out of him."

"That's easy," Mitch from Norfolk, Virginia, says. "My father believed in karma and he always said, 'What goes around, comes around.' One time we were broke down by the side of the road and he tried to flag down a truck. It passed right by us and he said, 'What goes around, comes around.' Turns out our coil had a faulty connection, which he easily fixed. Once we got back on the road, that same truck was stuck with a flat not five miles away. When we passed it, he waved."

"I still ride with my father every chance I get," Mike from Medford, Oregon, says. "He has two sayings that have become family jokes, but both are true. One has to do with the need to get out and ride: 'It usually takes a whole tank of gas before you start thinking straight.' The other is a classic and is just generally good advice for bikers everywhere. It goes, 'The only good view of a thunderstorm is from your rearview mirror.' Amen to that."

"My father spoke very little," Jeff from Anderson, South Carolina, told me. "But I learned from his actions and he was always working on a couple of bikes for himself and his brothers. Two days before he died he finished and started up a 1965 Pan he had been working on for more than a year. He and I listened to that sweet motor and he let me ride it around our property. When I came back and shut off the bike, he said, 'Well, that's that.' He died of a massive heart attack just two days later. I spoke at his eulogy and told that story. It was as if he knew the end was near. 'That's that.' He taught me to be true to myself above all else and to always finish what I start."

KICK STARTING YOUR LIFE

My father was not a biker, but my older sister married one. I'll never forget being a kid and hearing the sound of a pack of Harleys descending on our home. It was a sound like thunder; biker/songwriter Harry Fryed calls it the sound of dirty thunder. I like that. I recall seeing those gleaming Harleys riding up the street in perfect precision, how their riders flicked them around and backed them to the curb and how all that cacophony of dirty thunder suddenly stopped when they shut the bikes down in unison.

I would watch them get off their bikes and I remember thinking, "Someday, I'm going to be one of them." Though my parents were horrified, the day came when I had my own motorcycle and I started down the long road known as the school of hard knocks that teaches many of the lessons of the One Percenter Code.

> I recall seeing those gleaming Harleys riding up the street in perfect precision, how their riders flicked them around and backed them to the curb and how all that cacophony of dirty thunder suddenly stopped when they shut the bikes down in unison.

When I was a kid, there were still small mom-and-pop motorcycle shops where a boy could hang out and learn a thing or two about how to repair motorcycles and learn how to be a righteous biker. I remember riding my bicycle to such a shop after school almost every day when I was around 14. It was a very small shop and the owner made most of his money selling used bikes and wrenching on customers' rides. I think he only had one employee, a tattooed biker in the great 1970s tradition of hippy bikers. I must have driven those poor guys nuts with all my questions. But back then, the only way to apprentice to be a biker was to show up at a shop like that and sweep the floors until the owner noticed you.

I know a lot of older bikers can relate to this. I've asked quite a few if they have fond memories of such a shop, and many of them do. Invariably, the shop owner is a laid-back but sometimes cantankerous character who runs a shop because he loves motorcycles and not because he's out to make a fortune. Hanging out at that shop in North Miami Beach, Florida, I learned how to diagnose problems in a Harley motor just by listening to it. I was taught how to "read" sparkplugs to know how the motor was running. I learned how to trace down a short in the wiring system and how to check to make sure that the motorcycle was getting the three things it needed to start: gas, air, and spark.

I also learned a few things about rules of the road and rules about life along the way. The owner even let me ride his old Sportster a few

> "If you can kick start it,
> kid, you can ride it."

times. "If you can kick start it, kid, you can ride it." That's a great incentive for learning how to kick start a Harley and a great parable about life in general—if you have the balls to do what it takes to succeed, the world is your oyster.

The only time I had a problem with that Sportster was when I stopped by to show the sleek sled off to my girlfriend one afternoon and made the mistake of shutting the bike off . . . and then couldn't get it started. Bummer! I had to call the shop owner and explain the problem. I remember he laughed and told me that the bike had very little fuel in it and was on reserve. He said that when it got that low, the only way to kick start it was by sitting the bike upright so the gas would flow to the carb. That Sporty leaned waaaay over to the left on its jiffystand and the little bit of gas that was left couldn't get to the motor.

I quickly learned how to kick start a Harley while standing it upright (not an easy task), and having lost face in front of my girlfriend and the shop owner, I got it to kick over, blasted to the closest gas station, and filled that baby up!

SHOW 'EM WHO'S BOSS

By the time I was able to buy myself a used motorcycle by saving up all the money I made cutting neighbors' lawns (back then in Florida, they let you get your beginner's driver's license for small horsepower motorcycles at age 15), I was primed and ready to ride.

The only kind of Harley-Davidsons a teenager could afford back in the 1970s were used Shovelhead Sportsters, old FL Panheads, or maybe one of those little 350cc Sprints that Harley imported from

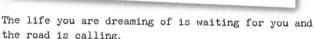

The life you are dreaming of is waiting for you and the road is calling.

Italy. I had a Sprint for a couple of years, and though it was small, it had the Harley logo on the gas tank and I thought I was the coolest kid on the block. In most of those cases, you had to learn to kick start your bike if you wanted to ride. Learning a motorcycle's specific personality in the starting procedure is a lot like learning how to please a woman. They are all different and they all like to be tickled in different ways to get their motors runnin'.

My third Harley was a piece-of-crap early generator Shovel that had been put in a rigid frame and was a real pisser to start. At first, I would walk out of the house on a winter day with a couple of layers of shirts on under my leather jacket and a wool scarf wrapped around my neck. I'd wheel the chopper out of the garage, turn on the gas, keep the ignition switch off, prime the old SU carburetor, kick it through twice, then flip the switch on, crack the throttle a quarter turn, and kick it to life with a roar of dirty thunder . . . unless it wouldn't start.

It was the kind of bike that if you didn't get the starting formula down to a science and it didn't roar to life on that first kick, you would be out there kicking for half an hour. Off came the scarf and the leather jacket. Then off came the shirts until I was just standing there in a sweaty T-shirt, kicking and cursing.

Then I met an old graybeard biker named Deacon Dave Phillips who made money by doing pinstriping by hand. He taught me a few secrets to kick starting an old Harley that are also life lessons. I rode over to his pad in Burbank, California, one day and was taking pictures of him doing pinstriping on a gas tank for a magazine article. He was a real character and a genuine old-school biker. He loved to play the guitar and sing, do paintings that portrayed the biker lifestyle, and offer up roadworthy wisdom to young upstarts such as myself. His custom chopper was as wild as the man himself, sporting a 16-inch overspringer front end, a stroked Panhead motor, a king and queen seat, and bars-to-the-stars apehangers. He called the bike "Ego Trip" because he did a plaster cast of his face and turned it into part of the peanut gas tank so that when he looked down at the tank, he was looking at himself!

He was such a character that I decided to do a video documentary on him. So one afternoon, I was over at his pinstriping joint and I let the videotape roll. I remember that I asked him, "How do you know if you're a biker?"

Deacon thought for a minute, smiled, and said, "Well, when you wake up in the morning next to your ol' lady and look over at her, your first thought is of her. But if your second thought is, 'I wonder if that ol' bike of mine is gonna start this morning,' you're probably a biker."

I'll never forget the lesson in kick starting my bike that he gave me one afternoon. I was getting ready to leave his place and that old Shovelhead just wouldn't start. Deacon came out and sniffed the bike. "It's not flooded," he crooned and pushed me out of the way. Then he did something that went completely counter to what I had been taught about starting a motorcycle. He twisted the throttle

As I put on my leathers, Deacon slapped me on the back and said, "Ya gotta show 'em who's boss, kid."

open all the way, left it open, and kicked the bike. It made that weird "woof" sound that old Shovels make when they're tryin' to start. He held the throttle all the way open and kicked it again and damned if it didn't start right up. He played with the throttle, blipping the motor to keep it running, then let it lope into that classic low idle "ka chunk, ka chunk, ka chunk" that Shovelheads are known for.

As I put on my leathers, Deacon slapped me on the back and said, "Ya gotta show 'em who's boss, kid." And you know what? He was right, and what's more, life is like that. You've got to take the bull by the horns. Sometimes, the best way to get through something is to give it the gas and the best way to live life is full throttle!

8.
MEDIA
WARS

**THE MEDIA MYTH
CREATED ABOUT THE
OUTLAW BIKER COMPARED
TO THE TRUTH ABOUT WHO ONE
PERCENTERS REALLY ARE**

> "What is a rebel?
> A man who says no."
>
> —Albert Camus

Every second of every day, we Americans are bombarded with all forms of media manipulation. This is mostly done in an attempt to get us to buy a lot of stuff we don't really need. From TV, radio, newspaper, and Internet advertising to product placement in movies and TV shows, to smartphone imbedded ads and clever store shelves that lure you to products, we are up to our eyeballs in media manipulation. This clever form of brainwashing is also used to condition the masses, teaching us how to think, what to think, and how to react, and it is used, for the most part, to keep us docile and compliant.

How does this corporate-controlled reality affect bikers and others of a decidedly rebellious bent? Media manipulation is used to great effect to make the population believe that anyone who does not toe the company line of obedience is a wild card and must be snuffed out. We are all taught that anyone who has the audacity to think his or her own thoughts (God forbid) is a renegade, a maverick, a rebel of the worst kind, may very well be insane, and is extremely dangerous to society. Therefore, the vast majority of what has been written or presented, whether through TV commercials or documentaries, biker movies, magazine or newspaper articles, and books about one percenter motorcycle clubs has been a load of absolute rubbish.

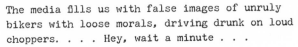
The media fills us with false images of unruly
bikers with loose morals, driving drunk on loud
choppers. . . . Hey, wait a minute . . .

The following joke offers the perfect example of how the media
tries to sell us on the idea that we should all fear bikers:

A biker is riding by the zoo when he sees a little girl leaning into
the African lion's cage. Suddenly, the lion grabs her by the cuff
of her jacket and tries to pull her inside to slaughter her while her
screaming parents watch, immobilized with fear. The biker jumps
off his bike, runs to the cage, and hits the lion square on the nose
with a powerful punch.

Whimpering from the pain, the lion jumps back, letting go
of the girl, and the biker carries her to her terrified parents, who
thank him profusely.

> The vast majority of what has been written or presented, whether through TV commercials or documentaries, biker movies, magazine or newspaper articles, and books about one percenter motorcycle clubs has been a load of absolute rubbish.

A newspaper reporter has seen the whole scene, and, addressing the biker, says, "Sir, that was the most gallant and brave thing I have ever seen a man do in my entire life."

"Why, it was nothing," the biker drawls. "Really, the lion was behind bars. I just saw this little kid in danger and acted as I felt was right."

"Well, I'll make sure this won't go unnoticed," the reporter says. "I'm a journalist, you know, and tomorrow's paper will have this on the front page. What kind of motorcycle do you ride?"

"A Harley-Davidson," the biker says, proudly.

The next morning, the biker picks up the newspaper to see if the reporter has kept his word and there, plastered across the front page, is the blazing headline:

BIKER GANG MEMBER ASSAULTS AFRICAN IMMIGRANT AND STEALS HIS LUNCH.

BIG BROTHER

Today's mainstream media is ridiculously obvious in its inherent bias and manipulation. If you don't believe me, check out Fox News. Believe me, if a network has to say that its reporting is "fair and unbiased," you are no doubt being lied to. The American media is owned directly by large multinational corporations, and through

Rebels of all kinds do not fit into the program; we
are round pegs that the system is trying to shove
repeatedly into square holes.

their boards of directors, they are connected with other major global
corporations and elite interests. An example of these connections
can be seen through the board of Time Warner.

Time Warner owns *Time* magazine, HBO, Warner Brothers, and
CNN. The board of directors includes individuals affiliated with the
Council on Foreign Relations, the International Monetary Fund,
the Rockefeller Brothers Fund, Warburg Pincus, Phillip Morris, and
AMR Corporation, and many others.

Two of the most "esteemed" sources of news in the States are
The New York Times and the *Washington Post*. *The New York Times*
has on its board people who have been or are presently affiliated
with Schering-Plough International (pharmaceuticals), the John
D. and Catherine T. MacArthur Foundation, Chevron Corporation,
Wesco Financial Corporation, Kohlberg & Company, The Charles
Schwab Corporation, eBay Inc., Xerox, IBM, Ford Motor Company,
and Eli Lilly & Company, among others. The same can be said for the
Washington Post, which has on its board the following: Lee Bollinger,
the president of Columbia University and chairman of the Federal
Reserve Bank of New York; Warren Buffett, chairman and CEO of
Berkshire Hathaway; and individuals associated with the Coca-Cola

Company, New York University, Conservation International, the Council on Foreign Relations, Xerox, Catalyst, Johnson & Johnson, Target Corporation, RAND Corporation, General Motors, and the Business Council. Doesn't sound like a very impartial group, does it? This is a group with one idea and aim at heart, namely, to make the world safe for capitalism and consumerism.

Naturally, rebels of all kinds do not fit into the program; we are round pegs that the system is trying to shove repeatedly into square holes. When you think of the media's portrayal of a one percenter motorcycle club, you might picture a group of organized thugs in leather—sort of a chopper-riding Mafia that deals in drugs, guns, and prostitutes. The motorcycle clubs of the 1940s and '50s were the very opposite of that image. These were fun-loving guys who were out to taste a little of the freedom they had fought so hard to win during World War II. Most of them were vets, for God's sake. They bled so that Americans could continue to enjoy their Cheerios every morning. They were not out to destroy the country they worked so hard to defend.

Media coverage of the so-called Hollister riot started antibiker sentiments in America after the July 1947 issue of *Life* magazine blew the whole incident way out of proportion. After that, citizens began looking over their shoulders to see if their town would be the next burg to be vandalized by crazed, motorcycle-riding hooligans. The media had a new threat to promote, and this one came from within our borders—just the thing to sell newspapers.

The American media is owned directly by large multinational corporations, and through their boards of directors, they are connected with other major global corporations and elite interests.

Of course, the Hollister incident wasn't the only reason that magazines and newspapers grabbed onto the idea that there was money to be made exploiting the bad boy image of one percenters. The quiet town of Riverside, California, hosted two post-Hollister bike events—one on Labor Day in 1947 and another on the Fourth of July in 1948. These two events are often lumped together as wild orgies of street racing, drinking, and fighting, but it was the July 4 party in Riverside that made all the newspapers.

CYCLISTS TAKE OVER TOWN

The headline from the local Riverside newspaper screamed: CYCLISTS TAKE OVER TOWN. Supposedly, more than 2,000 bikers took over the town and rode wildly in the streets. According to the article, "With one dead and 54 arrested in the second outbreak of rowdyism [yes, "rowdyism"] from motorcyclists in 11 months, Sheriff Carl F. Rayburn said he will sponsor no more motorcycle races in Riverside."

Even the local police could not accept this wildly sensational bit of journalism, and on July 17, 1948, the Riverside Sheriff's Department released an open letter to the press and public to put the rumors of rowdy bikers and riots in the street to rest. The extent of the damage caused by motorcycle hoodlums that weekend? An awning got torn down, a bottle was dropped out a hotel window, a

Even the local police could not accept this wildly sensational bit of journalism, and on July 17, 1948, the Riverside Sheriff's Department released an open letter to the press and public to put the rumors of rowdy bikers and riots in the street to rest.

Outlaw clubs of the 1940s and 1950s set the style
bikers would follow from that point on.

man's wallet was stolen, and three motorcycles were stolen, and one
of them was recovered.

According to Robert Abbott, the undersheriff who wrote the
letter, the news media blew the above activity into "a weekend of
terror, resulting from an invasion of Riverside by hoodlums and their
molls on motorcycles rioting in the streets and wrecking the city."
Abbott said that in order to cinch the matter, and to make sure the
wire services would carry the story to the entire nation, the news
article added the spicy bit that "the invasion left 54 arrested and
one killed."

The undersheriff commented that that one person killed in all of
Riverside County that weekend ran into a bridge abutment nearly
100 miles away from the town of Riverside and that the death
had nothing whatsoever to do with the rally. As a matter of police
record, there were no traffic accidents in the City of Riverside from
Saturday afternoon on July 3, until Monday afternoon at 1:15
p.m., motorcycle or otherwise. Not a bad record for a township of
50,000 inhabitants.

Abbott stated, "To say that the news services have been guilty of
gross exaggeration and sensationalism in their presentation of this

Fourth of July weekend and last Labor Day weekend in Riverside is an understatement."

Even in the wake of the media-induced hysteria caused by Hollister, Riverside, and later with Stanley Kramer's 1954 film *The Wild One*, the Boozefighters and other motorcycle clubs that burned rubber on the highways were still basically "drinking clubs with motorcycle problems." They were fairly tame at the time when compared with what would soon follow.

BIKERS ARE OUT TO RAPE YOUR DAUGHTERS

The next big antibiker media blitz was centered around an incident that occurred during Labor Day weekend in 1964. Hells Angels and other one percenter clubs from chapters all over California were having a run up to Monterey to raise funds to send a fallen brother's body home for burial. Members of the Oakland chapter of the HAs roared up through Monterey, right through the middle of town, and parked at a big tavern known as Nick's. By three in the afternoon more than 50 bikes were parked out front, like horses tethered and waiting faithfully before some Wild West saloon.

As the story goes, two girls—one white and pregnant, the other black—and their boyfriends were hanging out and drinking with the club. Local police provided a secluded stretch of beach for the Angels to camp on and the party eventually moved to the desolate dunes between Monterey Bay and Fort Ord. The cops even posted a guard on the highway to keep the Angels from taking the party back to town.

The so-called "victims" of this encounter later told police that they went to the beach from Nick's because they wanted to see all the cyclists. The two girls and five male friends joined the party around a roaring bonfire. Club members at the scene remember the girls as being wasted when they arrived. Wine flowed; there was talk and laughter. Soon the girls asked to get high and walked away from the fire with a few bikers. Apparently, one of the girls' boyfriends got scared and went for the cops.

By early morning, a roadblock sealed the beach and the two women sat in the back of a police car, pointing out which of the bikers present had supposedly raped them. As you can imagine, the newspapers had a field day with this one. California newspaper headlines blasted the Hells Angels for allegedly gang raping two minors (supposedly 14 and 15 years old) repeatedly. What did not make the papers was that medical examiners reported that neither of the girls had actually been raped. Seems like an important omission. Interestingly, the rape case was not front-page national news to begin with. Journalists at the time were focusing on the national election story. It wasn't until Attorney General Thomas C. Lynch released a 15-page report condemning outlaw bikers that the national media picked up the torch.

Within a few months of the incident, major stories by such media giants as *The Saturday Evening Post*, *Time*, *Newsweek*, and *The New York Times* helped create the image of the Hells Angels and other one percenter motorcycle clubs as degenerate monsters on wheels. The HAs went from obscurity to being the focus of a modern witch hunt in nothing flat. Suddenly, reporters came out of the woodwork to get an interview with a real Angel. At about the same time, gonzo journalist Hunter S. Thompson was spending a lot of time with the Oakland chapter of the Angels. He would later turn his encounters into an article for *The Nation* (May 17, 1965) called "Motorcycle Gangs: Losers and Outsiders." Thompson chronicled his experiences with the Hells Angels in his book, *Hell's Angels: The Strange and Terrible Saga of the Outlaw Motorcycle Gangs*.

While Thompson's sensationalized book turned more than a few straight stomachs with its look at the raunchy side of the biker

> What did not make the papers was that medical examiners reported that neither of the girls had actually been raped. Seems like an important omission.

lifestyle, it also was the inspiration for many guys in their teens and twenties to go out and buy a motorcycle. For while Hunter Thompson's sneak peek inside a one percenter motorcycle club ends on a sour note (the HAs end up having to thump Hunter a little bit), the mental picture he painted of the unbridled thrills of jammin' down the highway on a chopped Harley sure made many young men want to get out on the highway and ride.

NO SYMPATHY FOR THE DEVIL

Just as with the Hollister and Riverside incidents, the media used the Monterey rape case to sell papers, magazines, and books. In the process, it made the Hells Angels famous. Naturally, with fame comes more fame, or infamy, and it didn't take long for motion picture producers to catch on to the latest exploitable sensation. Soon the B-movie industry was cranking out dozens of cheap, exploitation biker films. The portrayal in these films of all bikers as some sort of devil spawn did nothing to help the one percenter image, which continued to degrade in the 1960s. Naturally the public, being mindless sheep, accepted whatever the media told them and were happy to have something new to feel superior to.

Bad biker movies were a hit at drive-ins in those flower power days of the '60s and certain one percenter motorcycle clubs continued to show up in the press, and never for doing something nice. While there was a brief time when hippies and acid-heads

We are not about what we buy and what we own; we are about who we are inside.

invited Hells Angels to parties in Haight-Ashbury, this came to sudden end when a group of HAs disrupted a peace march in 1965. The Oakland chapter even contacted President Lyndon Johnson and offered to go to Vietnam and fight as a "crack group of fighting guerillas." But all this was just a prelude to an incident that would make major headlines due to its mix of rock superstars and murder.

On Saturday, December 6, 1969, the Rolling Stones were set to play Altamont Speedway in Northern California and the Oakland Chapter of the Hells Angels, led by the charismatic Sonny Barger, had been asked to provide security for the band. It was late in the day and all the opening bands, such as Santana; Crosby, Stills, Nash and Young; and Jefferson Airplane had already played and left the stage. As the sun set, the Stones were taking their time, making the massive crowd of more than 300,000 fans wait to see them. The crowd got very angry and went crazy when the Stones finally came out, surging into the security barrier in front of the stage. The Hells Angels pushed the crowd back and off the stage and they used shortened pool cues as persuaders.

Then somebody threw a bottle at an Angel, followed by more bottles being thrown. The angry crowd had the audacity to start

> When the smoke cleared,
> an Angel had been shot by
> Meredith Hunter, but that
> fact is seldom remembered.

messing with the Angels' bikes, which were parked in front of the stage area. It doesn't take a genius to tell you that messing with a one percenter's bike is a very bad idea. The Angels entered the crowd, grabbed a few of the vandals, and started beating them down.

A black man in a bright green suit rushed the stage and pulled out a gun. Mick Jagger was singing "Under My Thumb" when Meredith Hunter got up on the stage. He was knocked off the stage before the gun went off. In the melee that ensued, the man got stabbed and the Angels picked him up and handed him over to the medics. When the smoke cleared, an Angel had been shot by Hunter, but that fact is seldom remembered. Hunter died of his wounds, and the press had a field day with the riot at Altamont. Once again, the Hells Angels were seen as monstrous devils, and critics called the tragedy the "Death of the Woodstock Nation."

Soon after this event, bikers began to turn up as the bad guys on television shows, taking the place of Wild West outlaws. Being a biker was no longer a wholesome pursuit, according to the mass media. We became the people that your mother warned you about. Many one percenter clubs did nothing to help this notion, reveling in their infamy.

So many myths and legends have grown up around one percenters in the past 50 years that it is nearly impossible to separate fact from fiction. But of all the biker exploitation films made from the 1960s to today, two really stand out in my mind as going way over the deep end to make one percenters into the devil's minions.

The 1990 film *Another 48 Hours* starred Eddie Murphy and Nick Nolte (reprising their roles from the original *48 Hours*) as unlikely undercover cop partners out to stop a group of one percenters who are so badass that they only stop short of being undead vampires in their unholy lust for blood and carnage.

The 1991 testosterone-laced *Stone Cold* featured hunky ex–Seattle Seahawk Brian Bosworth as a cop who goes undercover in a one percenter motorcycle club known as The Brotherhood, led by Lance Henrikson (who was the bright spot in this picture as Chains). Here the media's idea of one percenters being some vast underground two-wheeled Mafia is complete with drug and arms running, prostitution, and even political murders for fun and profit.

Both of these films paint one percenters as the most dark and twisted of creatures. Next to these bikers, Hannibal "The Cannibal" Lechter appears to be a member of *La Cage Aux Folles*. Such movies were conjured by Hollywood writers thanks to the media perception that one percenter motorcycle clubs are all involved in organized crime.

CRACKDOWN

Law enforcement agencies have long believed that one percenter motorcycle clubs are complex criminal organizations. The problem for them is that proving a club's tie to organized crime is extremely difficult and demands major funding for long-term investigations. The RICO Act was used in the 1970s and '80s in an effort to shut down the drug trade. Hells Angels Oakland Chapter president Sonny Barger was arrested on conspiracy and drug charges in 1979 (Sonny has also held the post of the HA's national president). Naturally, the press had a field day with Sonny's arrest; the story made it to *Time* and *Newsweek* magazines with the usual exaggerations. Ever notice that if a one percenter is arrested and they raid his pad and find a hunting knife and a pellet gun, the report mentions confiscating "a large arsenal of weapons"?

This particular case was a media circus lasting eight months. The court demanded that bulletproof glass be installed in the courtroom and that everyone in or out of the building be searched for weapons. Defense attorneys made the point that the RICO Act is unconstitutional since a club cannot be held accountable for the actions of every member. When the case was concluded in July 1980, news

> Ever notice that if
> a one percenter is arrested
> and they raid his pad and find
> a hunting knife and a pellet
> gun, the report mentions
> confiscating "a large
> arsenal of weapons"?

magazines failed to report that after 17 days the jury could not reach a verdict on 32 of the 44 counts against Sonny, his wife, Sharon, and a few others. And the cost to taxpayers after all this wasted time and effort? Try something in the neighborhood of five million dollars. Yes indeed, your tax dollars at work.

Over time, the RICO Act had decimated one percenter motorcycle clubs. Many patch holders were in prison, often on trumped-up charges, others went into hiding, and some clubs collapsed entirely.

YOU MEET THE NICEST PEOPLE ON A . . . HARLEY?

When Harley-Davidson came out with its Evolution motor in the mid-1980s and white-collar workers took to riding new Harleys in droves, many one percenter clubs were changing their image. Motorcycle clubs began getting involved with local charity projects, showing a new face to the public and to the media. If they were to survive, one percenters had to educate the public and prove that being a member of a motorcycle club did not make you public enemy number one.

Eventually, the media perceived this shift in outlaw attitude and reported on it. In 1990, the *Los Angeles Times* offered a headline that read, "Hells Angels Make Good Neighbors in Ventura." The piece had to do with the club's ability to coexist with locals and mentioned their efforts at raising money for local charities.

So much for the old slogan "You meet the nicest people on a Honda."

While American motorcycle clubs were learning to use the media to their advantage to promote a positive face to the masses, Europe and the rest of the world was a decade behind their U.S. counterparts with tough one percenter clubs taking the outlaw stereotype very seriously. Foreign papers reported clubs shooting up and bombing rival clubhouses.

Then, just as the American media seemed to be making nice with the outlaw image of one percenters, an incident took place that was far more deadly than Hollister, Riverside, Monterey, and Altamont put together.

THE LAUGHLIN SHOOTOUT

The outlaw world is never quiet. Somewhere, some one percenter motorcycle club is always at war with a rival club. This is nothing new; one percenter motorcycle clubs have fought each other for turf since there have been one percenter clubs. These biker wars have ranged from street rumbles, bare-knuckle fights, and knifings in the best *West Side Story* tradition, to all-out warfare with guns and even

> No one expected the
> bloodshed that took place
> under the bright lights of a
> famous gambling casino when
> two rival clubs suddenly
> went toe to toe.

bombings of rival clubhouses. Normally one percenter motorcycle clubs handle their battles in private, in dark places, away from public scrutiny. But no one expected the bloodshed that took place under the bright lights of a famous gambling casino when two rival clubs suddenly went toe to toe. The little desert gaming town of Laughlin, Nevada, was in no way prepared for the shootout that occurred on Saturday, April 27, 2002.

The Mongols and the Hells Angels had been keeping an uneasy peace before 2002's annual Laughlin River Run, where more than 40,000 mostly rich urban riders on high-dollar Harleys showed up for a weekend of gambling, partying, and riding. According to law enforcement intelligence, which is usually gathered by informants within the clubs, reports indicated the Mongols intended to bolster their status by attacking members of the Hells Angels.

A genuine Wild West shootout inside Harrah's Laughlin Casino left three dead and dozens wounded. According to a report in the *Las Vegas Review-Journal*, one of the dead was a Hells Angel and one was a Mongol. By the way, no ordinary citizens were hurt. As stated in the arrest report, the casino had a matrix of video surveillance cameras covering the scene of the shootout and police were able to watch the tapes over and over again to try to figure out what happened. They were supposedly able to figure out who some of the shooters were and arrested one man in connection to the shooting. I have talked to insiders who have seen the tapes and some say that an undercover cop actually started the massacre by shooting first.

The violence in the casino occurred just hours after a Hells Angel was found shot to death in San Bernardino, California. Casino sources said that the HAs, who were hanging out at the Flamingo Hotel, got word of the shooting in Berdoo and rode over to Harrah's to confront the Mongols. The Flamingo was traditionally Hells Angels territory during the run as was Harrah's for the Mongols.

The fallout from the shooting dragged on for nearly a decade. On March 10, 2009, the *Las Vegas Review-Journal* newspaper reported that the legal battle over the 2002 Laughlin shootout was over due to the sentencing of the last Hells Angel who faced federal charges.

In all, 42 members of the Hells Angels Motorcycle Club were indicted on federal racketeering and firearms charges. Judge James Mahan dismissed charges against 36 Hells Angels after learning the government did not turn over all of its evidence to the defense team. Six other members of the motorcycle club had already received prison terms.

Frederick Donahue was a fugitive for five years before surrendering in Las Vegas in July 2008 and was sentenced to 30 months in federal prison. All plea deals were carefully worded to state that each biker acted as an enterprise made up of individuals, not members of the HAMC. This effectively eliminated The Red and White as a criminal enterprise, and all bikers avoided enhanced sentences.

OPERATION BLACK RAIN

In the past 30 years, the United States has carried out raids on every major one percenter motorcycle club in this country. Of all the instances I've heard of wherein U.S. law enforcement agencies spend millions of taxpayers' dollars to spy on, infiltrate, and collect information on one percenter motorcycle clubs, one of the all-time biggest travesties of justice has got to be what the Federal Bureau of Alcohol, Tobacco, Firearms and Explosives (ATF) called Operation Black Rain.

Thanks to media manipulation, the American people have been made to believe that Operation Black Rain, carried out in 2008 against The Mongols Motorcycle Club, was a big success against a criminal empire. This could not be further from the truth. As I've mentioned, most of the members of a one percenter motorcycle club today are family men, and many have professional occupations, including being doctors and lawyers. These are men who love to ride motorcycles and enjoy the brotherhood found in an MC. There is no super-secret sinister empire of doom such as the ATF would have you believe. The operation itself has become an enormous debacle and a sad commentary on what so-called law enforcement can get away with when no one stands up against them. Well, no one except for one percenters, that is.

Several undercover agents infiltrated the Mongols and over time became fully patched members, collecting data for more than three years before springing the raids that served more than 160 search warrants and 110 federal arrest warrants in California, Nevada, Washington, Ohio, Colorado, and Oregon. In San Gabriel Valley, California, alone, more than 1,000 heavily armed storm troopers conducted sweeps of clubhouses and personal residences. In a Nevada chapter they arrested 7 of 11 members. In Colorado, 10 of the 11 members, and in Oregon authorities made no arrests, but did issue several search warrants.

Over the years there have been many instances of undercover agents infiltrating one percenter motorcycle clubs and even becoming fully patched members, living with and befriending the bikers before

Members of the Boozefighters, one of the original one percenter clubs that sprang up after World War II.

selling them out and trying to send them to prison. High-profile examples of this includes Billy Queen's earlier infiltration of the Mongols and Jay Dobyns' infiltration of the Hells Angels. Both men have since made lucrative careers writing books and accepting lecture tours and speaking engagements about their infamous exploits.

The thing that makes Operation Black Rain really stand out in the history books is not the number of club members arrested or how the ATF managed to sneak its men into the club under deep cover, but the move by the government to seize the *intellectual property* of a motorcycle club. Yep, they actually tried to go after the Mongols' colors! U.S. Attorney Thomas O'Brien sought the ability for the U.S. government to "own" the motorcycle club's patch, its logos, trademarks, and assigns. Amazing! O'Brien wanted the right to stop any member of the Mongols from wearing his patch and hoped to take the colors right off the patch holders' backs; the very same colors that the club has owned since 1969.

On October 23, 2008, in an unprecedented court action, U.S. District Court Judge Florence-Marie Cooper granted an injunction that prohibited Mongols club members, their family, and associates from wearing, licensing, selling, or distributing the Mongols logo. Can you believe that shit?

Then about a year later, the court ruled that the government could not take the trademark and that the ATF has no right to go around confiscating patches or other items containing the mark from private citizens who are not under indictment. So the Mongols got to keep their patch and the Feds had to stop making searches and seizures on their colors.

On July 1, 2011, news agencies reported that U.S. District Judge Otis D. Wright "regrettably" ruled in favor of the Mongols Motorcycle Club in the first-ever government attempt to gain control of the club's identity through a court order.

"This patch is a central element of the identity of the gang. We're trying to dismantle a criminal organization and we're trying to use whatever tools we can to do it," a spokesman for the U.S. attorney's office in L.A. told the *Los Angeles Times* upon bringing the case in July. "In this case it shows our determination to go after this organization as a whole—top to bottom leadership—and after the proceeds of criminal activity."

But Judge Wright was resolved to rule for the Mongols MC versus the government because the 2008 racketeering indictment that sparked the initiative to strip the Mongols of its logo failed to mention the organization by name. "Wright granted the biker gang's petition and vacated a preliminary order of forfeiture," according to the Associated Press.

THIS JUST IN

Interestingly, other than the recent ruling in favor of the Mongols MC, there has been very little press regarding American one percenter motorcycle clubs in the past few years (though violence continues involving club rivalry in other countries). In fact, one of the only articles I was able to find on the subject was dated June 19, 2010, and by an online motorcycle magazine called *Clutch & Chrome*. It states that the U.S. attorneys for the Eastern District of Virginia representing the ATF, Neil H. MacBride and Rich Marianos, announced at a press conference that the national president and 26 other members and associates of the American Outlaw Association (Outlaws) motorcycle club were indicted by a federal grand jury.

The 50-page indictment painted a picture of the Outlaws motorcycle club as being a highly organized criminal enterprise with a defined, multilevel chain of command. The indictment charged leaders and patch holders in chapters including Wisconsin, Maine, Montana, North Carolina, Tennessee, South Carolina, and Virginia. The Outlaws were alleged to have engaged in violent racketeering activities with the intent to expand the club's influence and control various parts of the country against rival motorcycle clubs.

Violence erupted when some of the members of the Outlaws were being arrested following the announcement. In Maine, members were involved in a shootout with federal agents during an attempted arrest, with a club member killed in the exchange.

Scouring news sources from coast to coast, the only other report came from television station KGET serving Bakersfield, California. It was also dated June 2010 and involved a motorcycle rally being canceled due to the Kern County Sheriff's Department concern that "gang violence" might break out.

Apparently, two weeks earlier a couple of members of rival one percenter motorcycle clubs got into a fight in Oildale, where two of the bikers were stabbed and one of them died. The far-from-in-depth reporting stated that: "17 News spoke with a woman who hangs out with local outlaw bikers. She did not want to be identified. She said there hasn't been major violence between local clubs in nearly 20 years. 'I've never seen anything bad happen. The stabbing was a fluke event. It's too bad that this tragic event just ruins everything, all of our fun for everyone,' she said." Yeah, just imagine all the fun the dead biker missed out on.

The end of the news report is my favorite part. Get this: "But some in the public feel some clubs are still dangerous, as they have been for decades. 'Some of them are, and I don't want to name names, but, yes, some of them are just as dangerous as they were before,' Harley-Davidson rider Joe Blow [name changed to protect the mentally deficient] said.'" Nice reporting.

> The 50-page indictment painted a picture of the Outlaws motorcycle club as being a highly organized criminal enterprise with a defined, multilevel chain of command.

Okay, so more than 50 years of one percenter motorcycle clubs terrorizing America and this is all the dirt that the ever-seeking media bloodhounds and the goose-stepping steel-toed boot brigade of the ATF could come up with? Hey, maybe there isn't a problem after all. Maybe one perenter motorcycle clubs mind their own damned business for the most part. There's a concept.

So in all the years of harassing clubs and after spending tens of millions of taxpayer dollars, the ATF has failed to prove that motorcycle clubs are organized criminal enterprises. The same, however, can't be said of the ATF itself, which has recently become embroiled in an international criminal investigation. Since it doesn't relate to one percenters, I won't go into the details, but if you're interested in learning more, just Google "Operation Fast and Furious."

FEAR THESE ONE PERCENTERS!

So who are the one percenters that all Americans should be afraid of, anyway? Are they

    (A) tax-paying granddads who ride shiny Harley-Davidson motorcycles and spend their weekends raising money for charities?

    (B) war veterans who returned home to ride motorcycles and experience the freedoms this country has to offer?

    (C) biker husbands and fathers who work nine to five alongside the rest of us?

    or (D) all of the above?

No. I'm sure you've figured out that the answer is "none of the above." The one percenters we should all fear are, in fact, the upper 1 percent of Americans who are now taking in a quarter of the nation's income every year. According to an article on April 8, 2011, by Roger Ebert for the *Chicago Sun-Times*, greed is seen as a virtue in America. Mr. Ebert was not so much surprised by the greed of these one percenters, but mystified by the lack of indignation voiced from the 99 percent of us not part of this elite circle of greed and deception.

The Boozefighters were heavily involved in the boisterous party that became known as the Hollister riot, and they were the model for the fictional Black Rebels MC featured in *The Wild One*.

"Day after day I read stories that make me angry," Ebert says. "Wanton consumption is glorified. Corruption is rewarded. Ordinary people see their real income dropping, their houses sold out from under them, their pensions plundered, their unions legislated against, their health care still under attack. Yes, people in Wisconsin and Ohio have risen up to protest these realities, but why has there not been more outrage?"

You want outrage? How about the Wachovia Bank money-laundering scheme? According to an article in the *Guardian*, "The authorities uncovered billions of dollars in wire transfers, traveler's checks, and cash shipments through Mexican exchanges into Wachovia accounts." Meanwhile, the bank paid fines of less than 2 percent of its $12.2 billion profit in 2009, and no individual was ever charged with a crime. Again quoting the *Guardian* article, "More shocking, and more important, the bank was sanctioned for failing to apply the proper anti-laundering strictures to the transfer of $378.4 billion—a sum equivalent to one-third of Mexico's gross national product—into dollar accounts from so-called *casas de cambio* (CDCs) in Mexico, currency exchange houses with which the bank did business."

Roger Ebert's point regarding these dangerous one percenters is that we have all become numb to stories such as these, stories of extreme greed in which anyone with the guts to take what they can gets away with it and is even rewarded with bonuses for such piratical exploits. *Bloomberg News* reports: "J.P. Morgan Chase & Co. gave Chief Executive Officer Jamie Dimon a 51 percent raise in 2010 as the bank resumed paying cash bonuses following two years of pressure from regulators and lawmakers to curb compensation."

The *Wall Street Journal* reported, "$57,031. That's about what the average U.S. archaeologist made last year. It's also what J.P. Morgan CEO Jamie Dimon made every day of last year—$20.8 million total, according to the firm's proxy filing this week. Anyone who has doubts about the resiliency of Wall Street banks and brokerages should ponder that figure for a while. The J.P. Morgan board also spent about $421,500 to sell Dimon's Chicago home. And they brought back the big cash bonus, doling out $30.2 million in greenbacks to Dimon and his top six lieutenants."

Mr. Ebert goes on to tell us that while there is nothing wrong with the very American credo of working hard to generate financial

Original Boozefighter and Hollister veteran Wino Willie Forkner, the prototype for the outlaw biker.

> The one percenters who
> we should all fear are, in
> fact, the upper one percent of
> Americans who are now taking
> in a quarter of the nation's
> income every year.

success, "a fair day's work for a fair day's pay," what we are seeing being fostered on the public by the top 1 percent of Americans who have controlled all the wealth in recent years should shock us all awake to rebellion. And yet it does not.

"Consider taxes," he begs of us. "Do you know we could eliminate half the predicted shortfall in the national budget by simply *failing to renew* the Bush tax cuts? Do you know that if corporations were taxed at a fair rate, much of the rest could be found? General Electric recently reported it paid no current taxes. Why do you think that was? Why do middle and lower class Tea Party members not understand that they bear an unfair burden of taxes that should be more fairly distributed? Why do they support those who campaign against unions and a higher minimum wage? What do they think is in it for them?"

And yet, the majority of Americans sit behind their glowing flat-screen TVs, gazing blankly at what passes for entertainment, night after night, happy to become numb by the power of media manipulation. "Don't think," a little voice in our head says. "It will only hurt your brain. Let us tell you what to think."

That's not the one percenter way. The one percenter is always prepared and always ready to act. It's time to unplug and prepare. Remember to keep your pitchfork sharp, your torches lit, and your powder dry, because the fuse has been lit and the whole shithouse is about to go up in flames. As our old buddy Hunter Thompson used to say, "Today's pig is tomorrow's bacon."

STANDING TALL IN THE WORLD THAT IS TO COME

WHAT DOES THE FUTURE HOLD FOR THE ONE PERCENTER CULTURE?

What happens when we turn away from those who tell us what to think? What happens when we refuse to buy into the system that society pushes on us in order to be free, to be who we really are? Naturally, the conformists will see us as nonconformists, as rebels . . . as outlaws. As such, we become more than individuals; we become a powerful collective force because we dare to say no. That is exactly what "they" are afraid of, and that's why society and the ATF think we have to be watched.

While there are those who believe that renegades and rebels are the bane of a sane civilization, we are a nation made up of rebels. In fact, were it not for the rebellious act of separation from Mother England, these United States would not exist as a free republic. One percenters are among the last vestige of rebellion in a nation that has become filled with sheep. While the average citizen rolls over and plays dead when confronted by the Man, bikers dare to stare down the system in its one, unblinking electronic eye, fully prepared to pluck that eye out!

There is evidence all around us that would have us believe that rebellion is futile, that the system is so entrenched that the right of the one is fully absorbed by the group mind, and that the system rules without question. I am here to tell you that this is not the case. There is much evidence that we actually create our own reality. In fact, the concept that we create reality nanosecond by nanosecond is gaining momentum in the world of quantum theory. A recent article in the *London Times* offered the headline: "The World is Make-Believe." The article to which the headline referred states that the human brain creates its own version of reality, and the world we see around us is mostly make-believe, according to a top British scientist.

Professor Bruce Hood is exploring the limits of the human mind in a series of lectures for the Royal Institution of Great Britain, the oldest independent research body in the world.

The psychologist plans to induce false memories in audience members in order to demonstrate how easily people are distracted, in a bid to prove how we have less control over our own decisions and perceptions than we like to imagine.

"A lot of the world is make-believe. We're only aware of a fraction of what's going on," Hood told the *Times*. "We have this impression of an expansive panorama in front of our eyes, but all we are ever seeing is an area the size of our thumbs at an arm's distance. The rest is filled in, as the brain creates a stable environment."

In a reality of our own creation, the act of one person can outweigh the many, even in this strange new world we find ourselves living in. There are still Robin Hoods in our midst. One man can create something like WikiLeaks and bring giants to their knees just as David was reported to have slain Goliath so long ago.

When the one hero among us is victorious against the dragon of repression, it is called a myth, a story that is always happening and is as old as humankind. The power of the individual to create change

Bikers have become mythic characters in our social consciousness in the same way that cowboys of the early West have become legendary.

for the masses is a very important aspect of what scholar and author Joseph Campbell called the Hero's Journey.

In his lifelong study of how myths from around the world survive for thousands of years and continue to inspire us, Campbell spoke of what he called the *monomyth*. In his amazing book, *The Hero with a Thousand Faces*, he summarizes the monomyth:

> A hero ventures forth from the world of common day into a region of supernatural wonder: fabulous forces are there encountered and a decisive victory is won: the hero comes back from this mysterious adventure with the power to bestow boons on his fellow man.

THE ONE PERCENTER AS AN ARCHETYPE

The image of the American biker has become iconic; bikers are thought of as bigger-than-life, epic characters, sometimes cast as the villain, sometimes cast as knights on iron steeds. Bikers have

> Being a biker is a way of life, not merely a lifestyle based around a particular type of vehicle.

become mythic characters in our social consciousness in the same way that cowboys of the early West and pirates of the golden age have become legendary and mythic.

Many people would look around at where we are going as a society, take into account the eventual extinction of fossil fuels, and tell you that the age of the gasoline-powered conveyance with its internal combustion engine is drawing to a close, and with the end of that age, loud, gas-powered Harley-Davidsons and the bikers who ride them will go the way of the dinosaur.

However, the biker mentality is a point of view, whether the rebel in question is actively riding a motorcycle or not. Being a biker is a way of life, not merely a lifestyle based around a particular type of vehicle. The biker has become a mythic archetype, and as such, even when the concept of the modern-day one percenter has been delegated to the history books along with the Huns, the Visigoths, and the Vikings, they will live on in our imaginations and in the collective memory of humanity. As such, the biker culture and One Percenter Code will never die. The iconic one percenter will live as myth.

THE HERO'S JOURNEY

Since the image of the one percenter has become an archetype in modern mythology, bikers play a part in Joseph Campbell's monomyth in which every story ever told is patterned, whether the tale comes from ancient times or our latest movies. In fact, George Lucas has mentioned that Campbell's work was the inspiration for the overarching story plots of his *Star Wars* films. Who is the one percenter

Machiavelli said that a defining characteristic of
a functioning nation-state was a monopoly on the
use of organized violence. The Man doesn't fear one
percenters because we ride motorcycles; he fears us
because a loosely-organized coalition of motorcycle
clubs represents a threat to that monopoly.

in *Star Wars*? He is the reluctant hero, the mercenary, the rebel . . .
he is Han Solo. Think about it.

All stories in the monomyth follow a number of stages along the
journey. The reluctant hero starts in his ordinary world and receives
a call to enter an unusual world of strange powers and events
(Campbell called this *a call to adventure*). If the hero accepts the call,
the world he knows will be pulled apart and he will face tasks and
trials (Campbell called this *a road of trials*). He may have to face them
alone, or he may have assistance. Think Frodo in *Lord of the Rings*.

At the story's most intense point, the hero must survive severe
challenges, often with help earned along the journey. If the hero
survives, he or she may receive a great gift (Campbell called this
the *goal* or *boon*), which will result in the discovery of important
self-knowledge. The hero must then decide whether to return with
this boon (Campbell called this *the return to the ordinary world*),
often facing challenges on the way home. If the hero is successful in

The mythic persona of the one percenter fits within the reluctant hero profile in any number of today's books and films.

returning, the boon or gift may be used to improve, save, or change the world (Campbell called this *the application of the boon*).

The basic stages of the monomyth and its hero's journey may be seen in the epic stories of Osiris, Prometheus, and Odysseus as well as those of the Buddha, Moses, and Jesus Christ. The modern retelling and reinvention of such stories appear in everything from *Star Wars* and *The Matrix* to *Avatar* and the Harry Potter series of books and films. The creators of all these modern myths have mentioned Joseph Campbell's work as the inspiration for their particular hero's journey.

The mythic persona of the one percenter fits within the reluctant hero (or antihero) profile in any number of stories, books, and films. The basic biker archetype is synonymous with Clint Eastwood's man with no name from the Sergio Leone westerns *Fistful of Dollars*, *For a Few Dollars More*, and *The Good, the Bad, and the Ugly*. The same archetype is present as Kurt Russell's Snake Plissken in John Carpenter's futuristic *Escape from New York* and *Escape from L.A.* films. A similar road rebel is seen in all three *Mad Max* films with Mel Gibson even donning a Cycle Champ–style black leather jacket.

The list of biker archetype reluctant heroes run the gamut from Han Solo and Spider-Man to Ash in the *Evil Dead* movies and such nonconformists as Patrick McGoohan's Number 6 in *The Prisoner* TV series. Who can forget his impassioned rage against the system that holds him when he announces, "I will not be pushed, filed, stamped, briefed, debriefed, or numbered. My life is my own. I am not a number; I am a free man!"

EVERY STORY EVER TOLD

The various aspects of Joseph Campbell's monomyth follow the action of every movie ever made, beat by beat. Yes, every film ever made. If you don't believe me, check out Blake Snyder's excellent books on how to write screenplays for movies: *Save the Cat!*, *Save the Cat! Goes to the Movies*, and *Save the Cat! Strikes Back*. Here's an outline of the Hero's Journey (see if this sounds familiar when placed in context of . . . you pick the movie):

THE ORDINARY WORLD: The reluctant hero, uneasy, uncom-
   fortable or unaware, is introduced sympathetically so the
   audience can identify with the situation or dilemma. The hero
   is shown against a background of environment, heredity, and
   personal history. Some kind of polarity in the hero's life is
   pulling him in different directions and causing stress.
THE CALL TO ADVENTURE: Something shakes up the situation,
   either from external pressures or from something rising up
   from deep within, so the hero must face the beginnings of
   change. His life is thrown out of balance.
REFUSAL OF THE CALL: The hero feels the fear of the
   unknown and tries to turn away from the adventure, however briefly. Alternately, another character may express the
   uncertainty and danger ahead.
MEETING WITH THE MENTOR: The hero comes across a
   seasoned traveler of the worlds who gives him or her training, equipment, or advice that will help on the journey. (For
   instance, Obi Wan gives Luke his father's light saber.) Or the
   hero reaches within to a source of courage and wisdom.

CROSSING THE THRESHOLD: At the end of Act One, the hero commits to leaving the ordinary world and entering a new region or condition with unfamiliar rules and values. He steps into the adventure that awaits.

TESTS, ALLIES, AND ENEMIES: The hero is tested and sorts out allegiances in the special world.

APPROACH: The hero and newfound allies prepare for the major challenge in the special world.

THE ORDEAL: Near the middle of the story, the hero enters a central space in the special world and confronts death or faces his or her greatest fear. Campbell calls this the "dark night of the soul." Out of the moment of death comes a new life.

THE REWARD: The hero takes possession of the treasure won by facing death. There may be celebration, but there is also danger of losing the treasure again.

THE ROAD BACK: About three-fourths of the way through the story, the hero is driven to complete the adventure, leaving the special world to be sure the treasure is brought home. Often a chase scene signals the urgency of the mission.

THE RESURRECTION: At the climax, the hero is severely tested once more on the threshold of home. He or she is purified by a last sacrifice, another moment of death and rebirth, but on a higher and more complete level. By the hero's action, the polarities that were in conflict are resolved.

RETURN WITH THE ELIXER: The hero returns home or continues the journey, bearing some element of the treasure that has the power to transform the world as the hero has been transformed. Remember the end of *The Matrix*? Neo gains the ability to walk between the worlds of the Matrix and reality, gaining the ability to manipulate the program. He can even fly!

THE CODE LIVES

Why do all stories and movies follow the template of the Hero's Journey? Because the Hero's Journey is the human story writ large. It is your story; that's why you are interested in watching it unfold over and over again in infinite different versions, time after time.

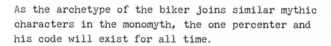

As the archetype of the biker joins similar mythic characters in the monomyth, the one percenter and his code will exist for all time.

It is our story as a people; every step into a new world, every dark night of the soul, every rebirth and triumph is a story about humanity, about who we are and where we're going. Simply put, the journey is *your* journey.

As the archetype of the biker joins similar mythic characters in the monomyth, the one percenter and his code will exist for all time. Even if the day comes when outlaw bikers as we know them become an extinct tribe, the One Percenter Code will live on just as the Code of the West and the knights' Code of Chivalry live on in our culture and just as the Hero's Journey lives on as the basis for our modern myths in books and movies. What's more, there is a very real need for the One Percenter Code today in an age in which we have all grown soft and complacent from having bought into the American consumer mindset.

The proud code of rebellion is a very American concept and is as wild and untamed as the West itself. Biker organizations across the country work tirelessly to monitor laws that would hamper our freedom and change our way of life, from the enactment of helmet laws to the restriction of off-road areas. *Easyriders* magazine started one of the biggest of these groups back in the 1970s. ABATE

> Even if the day comes when outlaw bikers as we know them become an extinct tribe, the One Percenter Code will live on just as the Code of the West and the knights' Code of Chivalry live on.

originally stood for A Brotherhood Against Totalitarian Enactments. These days the acronym has mellowed to become American Bikers Aimed Towards Education, the idea being that it is better to educate rather than legislate riders when talking about restrictive laws regarding motorcycling. As such, one percenters have learned to use the system to their advantage when possible, coexisting with the straight world on a daily basis.

The One Percenter Code and its rules of biker ethics will continue to be passed down from riding generation to generation, offering its freedom-oriented guidance to rebels yet to be born. Our young men and women need a code to live by and rites of passage that will indoctrinate them into their tribes and their communities. Now, more than ever, kids need a sense of belonging and a feeling of connection with their friends, their families, and their tribes. All human beings crave connection, and rites of passage provide that connection.

RITES OF PASSAGE

Basically, a rite of passage is an event—or series of events—that mark a person's progress or evolution from one station in life to another more profound and exalted position. While rites of passage are often thought of as "coming of age" rituals, they may also mark puberty, stepping into manhood or womanhood, marriage, and even death. Judeo/Christian religions use these rituals in the form of baptism, confirmation, and bar or bat mitzvahs.

Tribes have always used rites of passage as ways to mark the transition from childhood into adulthood and to bring young men and women fully into the tribe as accepted members. But there have also been various rites practiced for nearly every phase of life, from birth to death and every stage in between. We mark such occasions as birthdays, coming of age, marriage and divorce, and even changes in jobs. In fact, one of the modern practices for showing a transition in life is to mark it by getting a meaningful tattoo. In this way people mark their bodies with signs of transition and change.

One percenter motorcycle clubs mark rites of passage with each stage of becoming a member, from being accepted as a hang-around to becoming a prospect, to being a fully patched member and then possibly an officer in the club. As with stages of indoctrination in all groups of people, these rites of passage fall into three main phases: separation, transition, and incorporation.

In the separation phase, the participant is taken away from his familiar environment and former role and enters a very different

The biker code of rebellion is a very American concept and is as wild and untamed as the West itself.

> One percenter motorcycle clubs mark rites of passage with each stage of becoming a member.

and sometimes foreign routine he is forced to adjust to and become familiar with. A rite that would fall into this category would be birth. The infant leaves a very safe and secure environment in his mother's womb and enters an extremely different one in the real world. You also see this in the first stages of the Hero's Journey when the reluctant hero's life is thrown wildly out of balance and he finds himself in an unfamiliar world.

The transition phase is the time that the participant learns the appropriate behavior for the new stage he or she is entering. This phase can include the time when a person becomes engaged to be married. At this time, people are learning about the new stage of life they will soon enter. They are also adjusting and preparing for it, or making a transition. The transition phase may also include the time that children enter adolescence and leave their childhood behind. This is the time when people learn and grow and prepare to be independent adults in the real world. It is the prospecting phase of becoming a one percenter.

The last phase, incorporation, takes place when the participant is formally admitted into the new role. After people are married, they have taken on very new and different roles, having prepared for those roles in earlier transition and separation rites. For the one percenter, the incorporation phase marks the transition into becoming a fully patched member of a motorcycle club.

In the average life, there are many rites of passage. Some are more significant than others. Naturally, the big transitions we must all endure are birth, the transition from childhood to adolescence, then leaving home (perhaps for college), then marriage, then the birth of our own children, and finally death. Various cultures mark

It is the nonconformist who dares to ask the
hard questions and push humankind forward.
Even this guy.

these rites of passage in very different ways, and bikers have their
own special rites for such things as weddings, wherein the bride
and groom are dressed in riding attire and the presiding minister
(often the club president) has them place their hands on a Harley
shop manual. The groom is charged with such things as changing his
bride's oil every 5,000 miles. Prospects decorate the groom's Harley
for the getaway honeymoon and the wedding party makes sure that
every beer keg is drained to the last drop.

Biker funerals are also unique affairs and it's not unusual for a
one percenter to have hundreds of friends within the biker community attend his last rites to show respect. Motorcycle funeral proces-
sions are amazing affairs, with the sound of dirty thunder washing
over tombstones as bikes roll by two at a time in a seemingly endless
procession. There have been bikers who have been cremated and
had their remains stored in a Harley gas tank, or spread over a favorite stretch of road or at a particular bike rally, such as Sturgis. And
there have even been bikers who were buried with their precious
motorcycle to make sure they can still ride in Valhalla.

One of the ways children today can experience a rite of passage transition is through a vision quest. Native Americans and other indigenous peoples have used quests in the wilderness to mark transitions in life and to offer a spiritual rebirth since time out of mind. Such classes and workshops are available from many sources, including Circles of Air and Stone (www.questforvision.com), Wilderness Reflections (www.wildernessreflections.com), and Rites of Passage (www.ritesofpassagevisionquest.org).

YOU CAN'T KILL AN IDEA

What will become of the one perenter culture in a world that changes with alarming speed and complexity? As the character of V tells us in the film *V for Vendetta*, "You can't kill an idea." For the one percenter and those who will ride the highways of the future, that idea is rebellion. Look back in the history books and you will discover that whenever there has been a new frontier to explore, the first daring men who braved the unknown were one percenters. Imagine what it must have been like to throw yourself into the void with open hands and a mind seeking new borders.

Imagine the brave souls who set themselves adrift in wooden ships on endless oceans to travel beyond all the known maps in hopes of discovering what's out there. It has always been the one percenter in many lands and times who dared to go beyond what is known. We find ourselves in the same place today . . . stretching

> Look back in the history books and you will discover that whenever there has been a new frontier to explore, the first daring men who braved the unknown were society's one percenters.

fearlessly past all that is known. This is the special province of the one percenter.

As I mention in *One Percenter: Legend of the Outlaw Biker*:

In every case, once the map has been drawn and the great boundless frontier has been labeled, more people and cities follow and the wild ones are forced to move on. In the American West, wagon trains brought settlers farther and farther west. Steel tracks were soon laid from sea to shining sea and the locomotive brought men and women from many lands in search of a new way of life, new possibilities.

In every age, culture, and society, there is a need for the rebel. It is the nonconformist who dares to ask the hard questions and push humankind forward. It has always been so, and now we need new thought and new ideas more than ever before. After all, here we spin on a ball in space, six billion plus hominids, in transit from the world that was to the world that is becoming. Our planet is an incubator, seeking new visions to embrace a new greening.

No one can truthfully predict where humanity is going in the next hundred years and what the world of our great-grandchildren will be like, but I can guarantee you there will be one percenters. No matter what adventures unfold, the first men who dare to push into new worlds and new states of being will have the spirit of the one percenter riding with them. As such, it is my hope that future one percenters will look back at this book to find snatches of the code of conduct that forged a way of life for brothers and sisters of the road.

LIFE LESSONS

In researching this book, I asked one percenters from across the globe to tell me what they would like to leave behind for their children and their children's children. The following life lessons are presented in no particular order, but all are worth noting as part of the One Percenter Code.

Circumstances may have influenced who you are, but you're completely responsible for who you become.

Keep breathing in and out. The rest will take care of itself.

Change is constant and change is inevitable. Just remember that no matter what, this too shall pass.

The greedy and the rich die just like everybody else. The devil doesn't care what you drive.

When you're up to your neck in shit, keep your mouth closed.

It's not what you have in your life but *who* you have in your life that matters.

Circumstances may have influenced who you are, but you're completely responsible for who you become.

Most of the things you're looking for in life are right in front of you.

Bad things happen to everybody. You're not special in that regard. But it's what you do with the adversity in your life that tells you who you really are.

A motorcycle will never win an argument with a car.

No matter what you may think, time really does heal all wounds.

You either control your attitude or it will control you.

Trust in God . . . but lock up your Harley.

Sometimes people deserve a second chance . . . but never a third.

Personal glory lasts forever!

The world doesn't stop for your grief. Suck it up.

When you get old, you learn that all that stuff you heard about your health being really important *is* really important.

Everybody fails. It's the only way you learn how not to fail.

It may take years to build trust but only a second to destroy it.

One percenters do what has to be done, when it needs to be done, regardless of the consequences.

Don't be afraid to live life at full throttle!

Sometimes shit happens!

ONE PERCENTERS ALL!

Having learned much about the thoughts, actions, and deeds of one percenters, we realize that the One Percenter Code has always been with us. We hear the words of one percenters in the darnedest places because living life as a one percenter is a state of mind and a way of being. The One Percenter Code is etched into the American way as surely as the Code of the West. Now having heard a few important life lessons from one percenter bikers, I thought you might like to see some inspiring words of wisdom from other great minds. Examine these words and you'll find a bit of the one percenter in each who spoke them:

The bravest are surely those who have the clearest vision of what is before them, glory and danger alike, and yet notwithstanding go out to meet it. —*Thucydides*

Any fool can criticize, condemn, and complain, and most fools do. —*Benjamin Franklin*

Do what you can, with what you have, where you are. —*Theodore Roosevelt*

You can only lead others where you yourself are prepared to go. —*Lachlan McLean*

If you hit every time . . . the target is too near or too big.
    —*Tom Hirshfield*

Luck is what happens when preparation meets opportunity.
    —*Elmer Letterman*

Authority is 20 percent given and 80 percent taken!
    —*Kenneth Blanchard*

When the sea was calm all ships alike showed mastership in
    floating. —*William Shakespeare*

The task of the leader is to get his people from where they are
    to where they have not been. —*Henry Kissinger*

I am a great believer in luck, and I find the harder I work the more
    I have of it. —*Stephen Leacock*

But the whole thing, after all, may be put very simply. I believe
    that it is better to tell the truth than to lie. I believe that it is
    better to be free than to be a slave. And I believe that it is better
    to know than to be ignorant. —*H. L. Mencken*

Whenever I draw a circle, I immediately want to step out of it.
    —*Buckminster Fuller*

We make a living by what we get. We make a life by what we give.
    —*Winston Churchill*

All great ideas are dangerous. —*Oscar Wilde*

We must adjust to changing times and still hold to unchanging
    principles. —*Jimmy Carter*

In wildness is the preservation of the world.
    —*Henry David Thoreau*

Wounded people are dangerous; they know they can survive.
    —*Anonymous*

You cannot discover oceans unless you have the courage to leave the shore. —*Successories*

Lead, follow, or get out of the way! —*James Lundy*

To plunder, to lie, to show your arse are three essentials for climbing high. —*Aristophanes*

My center is giving way, my right is in retreat; situation excellent. I shall attack. —*Ferdinand Foch*

Experience has shown that even under the best forms those entrusted with power have, in time, and by slow operations, perverted it into tyranny. —*Thomas Jefferson*

Discovery consists of seeing what everybody has seen and thinking what nobody has thought. —*Albert von Szent-Gyorgy*

Where there is no vision the people perish. —*Proverbs 29:18*

We never do anything well until we cease to think about the manner of doing it. —*William Hazlitt*

Change your thoughts and you change the world.
—*Norman Vincent Peale*

Two roads diverged in a wood, and I . . . I took the one less traveled by, and that has made all the difference. —*Robert Frost*

It is better to die on your feet than to live on your knees.
—*Dolores Ibarruri*

Dictators ride to and fro upon tigers which they dare not dismount, and the tigers are getting hungry. —*Winston Churchill*

He who fears he will suffer, already suffers from his fear.
—*Michel Eyquen Montaigne*

Bikers tend to be the type of people who listen to that small, still voice within and carve out their own destiny.

Tyranny, like hell, is not easily conquered; yet we have this consolation with us, that the harder the conflict, the more glorious the triumph. —*Thomas Paine*

Fortune favors the brave. —*Terence*

We will either find a way, or make one. —*Hannibal*

When you win, nothing hurts. —*Joe Namath*

Re-examine all that you have been told . . . dismiss that which insults your soul. —*Walt Whitman*

All of life is on the wire; all else is waiting. —*Anonymous*

Treat people as if they were what they ought to be, and you will help them to become what they are capable of being. —*Johann W. von Goethe*

There is no limit to what can be accomplished when no one cares who gets the credit. —*John Wooden*

I am a revolutionist by birth, reading, and principle. I am always
  on the side of the revolutionists because there never was a
  revolution unless there were some oppressive and intolerable
  conditions against which to revolute. —*Samuel Clemens*

THE MAFIA CODE

Throughout this book I've mentioned a number of codes of conduct
from such positive role models as knights and cowboys, but you can
also see cues from the One Percenter Code being used in one of the
world's most notorious crime syndicates, the Mafia or *la Cosa Nostra*.
Some Italian friends of mine jokingly say that the word "Mafia"
stands for the Mothers And Fathers Italian Association.

In 2007, reports surfaced of a Ten Commandments of the Mafia,
uncovered from documents seized from the treasure trove of Cosa
Nostra heir Salvatore Lo Piccolo, who took over from kingpin
Bernardo Provenzano. The rules were drawn up to tamp down on
the young mafiosi infected with the John "Teflon Don" Gotti dis-
ease—mainly showing off in public—a real no-no for criminals who
favor a very low profile.

I include the Mafia's Ten Commandments here, not because I
believe there is any direct link between any biker club and the Cosa
Nostra, but simply because I thought you'd get a kick out of them.

The Ten Commandments of the Cosa Nostra:

No one can present himself directly to another of our friends.
  There must be a third person to do it.
Never look at the wives of friends.
Never be seen with cops.
Don't go to pubs and clubs.
Always being available for Cosa Nostra is a duty—even if your
  wife's about to give birth.
Appointments must absolutely be respected.
Wives must be treated with respect.
When asked for any information, the answer must be the truth.
Money cannot be appropriated if it belongs to others or to
  other families.

People who can't be part of Cosa Nostra: anyone who has a
close relative in the police, anyone with a two-timing relative
in the family, anyone who behaves badly and doesn't hold to
moral values.

THE ONE PERCENTER FUTURE

The one percenter ideal is a way of life and a point of view. As such,
I believe that the attitude expressed in the biker lifestyle transcends
current two-wheeled technology and will extend into whatever
brave new world that lies before us. The attitude of rebellion has no
bounds and no limits and the one percenter of the future will continue to write his own code and create his own maps.

Since I've interjected Joseph Campbell's Hero's Journey in this
chapter, I think it is pertinent to finish thoughts of the story of the
outlaw biker with Mr. Campbell's philosophy, which is often sum-
marized by his phrase: "Follow your bliss." He derived this idea from
the Upanishads (texts that were an early source of the Hindu religion). Campbell saw this concept as not merely a mantra, but a guide
to each of us, who are all on our Hero's Journey. He has been quoted
as saying, "If you follow your bliss, you put yourself on a kind of
track that has been there all the while, waiting for you, and the life
that you ought to be living is the one you are living. Wherever you
are, if you follow your bliss, you are enjoying that refreshment, that
life within you, all the time."

The attitude of rebellion
has no bounds and no limits
and the one percenter of the
future will continue to write
his own code and create
his own maps.

It's easy to see that this sort of philosophy fits within the One Percenter Code. Bikers tend to be the type of people who listen to that small, still voice within and carve out their own destiny. They are the captains of their life's ships, so to speak. One percenters live fully in the moment and live the lives they wish to live, moment by moment. No one knows what tomorrow will bring, but one percenters know that they can rely on their own philosophy and they can rely on their brothers in arms. Little else really matters. In an uncertain future, the One Percenter Code offers a standard to live by that keeps riders on the road.

10.
TAKING IT TO
THE STREETS

LIVING BY THE CODE
OF THE ONE PERCENTER
EVERY DAY

> "True brotherhood is the key to our survival and to our way of life. What matters is the strength of your heart and the love of your brothers."
>
> —Psycho, a one percenter

I can think of no better quote to begin this chapter on living the One Percenter Code every day of your life than the one above. Yet, what comes to many people's minds when they think of bikers? Some might instantly think of smelly, tattooed men with greasy hair astride very loud motorcycles. Hopefully this book has shown you that there are many sides to the image of the American biker and that there is more than meets the eye under all those black leather jackets. In fact, I've always thought that it's kind of funny to go to a massive motorcycle rally, such as the one held in Sturgis, South Dakota, every August, to witness a sea of black leather in 100-degree heat. This motorcycle mecca draws nearly 500,000 bikers every year and to see all those headbands and black T-shirts, you'd think that bikers are far from being individuals. The impression is that you're looking at some sort of convention in which people dress up to pretend to be bikers, and in fact, some do just that.

One percenters have placed their club first in their lives, and while this is a difficult thing to do sometimes, the benefits are that you are never alone. While girlfriends and wives come and go and friends and acquaintances drift in and out of your life, the club is always there, on good days and on bad. Your brothers always have your back. For some, that's enough, and for others, their club is all they need.

> One percenters have placed their club first in their lives, and while this is a difficult thing to do sometimes, the benefits are that you are never alone.

While many people continue to think of bikers in terms of the typical stereotype thug, others see bikers as free spirits, outlaws, and rebels who live their lives on their own terms each and every day. The One Percenter Code is all about living the life you want to live, being the person you want to be, and attracting to you the things that you want in your life. The essence of the code is that each of us is allowed to be an individual and live as free men and women. How do you live this code every day? One percenters know that there is a secret law that shows us how the universe works. Some call this the law of attraction.

THE LAW OF ATTRACTION

The concept of the law of attraction has been around for a very long time. Early references to this universal law cropped up in print during the New Thought movement (1904 to 1910). William Walker Atkinson wrote about the concept that "like attracts like" in his book *Thought Vibration or the Law of Attraction in the Thought World* in 1906. This was followed the next year by Bruce MacLelland's book *Prosperity Through Thought Force* and led to other books focusing on how to draw things to you, get rich, and be successful. The most famous of these was *Think and Grow Rich* by Napoleon Hill, first published in 1937. Hill's book certainly made him rich, with more than 60 million copies sold. His basic premise that you must control your thoughts in order to achieve success in life is also the basis for the hugely popular film *The Secret*.

Many people today had never heard of Napoleon Hill and the law of attraction until Rhonda Byrne's *The Secret* appeared in 2006 and spun off into a very successful book the following year. Both the film and book include interviews by such experts in the field of human potential as Jack Canfield, John Grey, Bob Proctor, Marci Schimoff, and Joe Vitale, whose book *The Key: The Missing Secret for Attracting Anything You Want* is a current bestseller. *The Secret* also features interviews with quantum physicists John Hagelin and Fred Alan Wolf.

This modern adaptation of the principles of the law of attraction supposes that our physical reality is actually a reflection of our thoughts, or, as quoted in *The Secret*, "your thoughts and your feelings create your life." Believe it or not, one percenters offer us a classic example of people living their lives in a fashion they created. Being a biker is a way of life you live every day. You get up in the morning and put your boots on the very same way, day after day, month after month, year after year. Being a biker is not a fashion show; it is who you are. Bikers are people who have consciously chosen the reality they live in and keep it real every day.

True brotherhood is the key to our survival and to our biker way of life.

While girlfriends and wives come and go and friends
and acquaintances drift in and out of your life,
the club is always there.

So how do we create the reality we choose to exist in? First, it is important to understand that the universe is neutral; it doesn't care what you create for yourself, but it is standing by to help you experience whatever you want, either in a positive or negative way. You've no doubt heard the old expression "Be careful what you wish for because you just may get it." Well, that certainly applies here.

One percenters and those who live the biker lifestyle have created a reality that fits with their freewheeling spirits. They aren't afraid to speak their minds and they stand up for what they believe in. They keep to the code every day of their lives.

You can create the reality you wish to live by simply changing your point of view. If you don't like your life, change it; all it takes is a thought. Specifically, it takes guided thought, and you have to set intention for what you want to attract in your life. While this idea sounds overly simple, it really is as easy (or as difficult) as that.

The problem that many people have when they do mantras or pray for something to manifest in their lives is that they're accidentally sending a negative wish out into the cosmos. For instance, if you wish to draw more abundance to you, your first thought might be to say: "I need more money." But putting that thought out there actually blocks you from getting the wealth you want. By saying, "I need more money," the universe basically says, "Okay, you need more money. Poof! You have the need for more money." So you just end up with having the need for more money and not the money you are trying to attract. In other words, if you don't understand how this law works, you can end up creating and attracting more of what you don't want.

According to those who believe in the law of attraction, the correct way to draw money to you is to intone a phrase such as, "I have infinite abundance in all things. Money and riches flow freely through me." By accepting this mantra and believing it as fact and feeling it and accepting it in every cell in your body, you instantly evoke the change you ask for. And the idea is that the law of attraction works for anything you wish to change in your life, whether it is that you're looking for the love of your life or that you wish to draw perfect health to you or you want to switch careers. You name it. Under this law, the world truly is your oyster.

Ask, believe, and you will receive. But how do you ask? What you believe and how you receive makes all the difference in whether you experience success or failure in utilizing the law of attraction. First you must define very clearly what it is you are going to ask for. You must have a very specific and clear goal in mind. Failing to have a clear goal is part of the "be careful what you wish for" part of this process.

For more information regarding the law of attraction and how it works, I suggest the excellent book *The Key* by Joe Vitale. Joe explains many of the problems that people encounter when they attempt to use the law of attraction. He tells us that you must be clear on what you want to attract and remove the blocks that you may have unintentionally placed in your way.

Being a biker is not
a fashion show; it is
who you are.

Ultimately, the real mystery to how everything works in this world, the real secret or key to success, is you. You have everything you need to be whatever you wish to be and to manipulate reality and manifest whatever you please. You just have to get out of your own way. As Neville Goddard wrote in his book, *The Power of Awareness*:

> You must assume the feeling of the wish fulfilled until your assumption has all the sensory vividness of reality. You must imagine that you are already experiencing what you desire. That is, you must assume the feeling of the fulfillment of your desire until you are possessed by it and this feeling crowds all other ideas out of your consciousness.

Bikers offer an excellent example of how the law of attraction works because they simply *are* the thing they wish to be. Don't dream it, be it. So if we can each be what we want to be and attract to us whatever we want, a natural progression of events takes place. Once you are happy with who and what you are and you have enough for yourself and your family, the next logical step is spreading this happiness to others. Bikers and

This man has either broken down or nature is calling. Given the lack of a giant puddle of oil beneath the Panhead, odds are it's the latter.

> Bikers and others who are comfortable in their own skin and content with who they are often turn to helping others and their community.

others who are comfortable in their own skin and content with who they are often turn to helping others and their community. More on that later.

KEEPING THE CODE

I believe there is a very real need to pass our knowledge down to our children and to give them a code to live by and rites of passage in order for them to be well-rounded human beings. Since starting this book, I have seen amazing proof of this. Recently, while at the Sturgis Motorcycle Rally, I asked lifelong one percenters from some of the world's most secretive and notorious motorcycle clubs to tell me what they taught their children in order to keep them on the straight and narrow path. What they told me may surprise you.

In every case, no matter how hardcore a biker their father was, the children of one percenters get a firm moral footing and, in some cases, learn from their fathers' mistakes, so that they grow into adults with excellent senses of value for themselves and for their own children. I was amazed at how many of the children of one percenters either are in college, are college graduates, or are professional people today. It did not seem to matter whether the one percenter's child decided to follow in his father's boots and ride motorcycles, become patch holders in motorcycle clubs, or to shun the lifestyle but take with him the important life lessons learned by his parents.

All the one percenters I spoke to for this book shared a quiet sense of gallantry. If you have ever spent time with a one percenter,

You reckon I can use that law of attraction thing to buy these here motorsickle parts?

you know what I'm talking about. One percenters, especially the officers of the clubs, have a nobility that reminds me of knights on iron steeds. They walk their walk and have nothing to prove to anyone. Who wouldn't like to follow in those engineer boots?

One graybeard biker I spoke to at Sturgis proudly pulled photos out of his chain wallet to show me his grown children: one son in Iraq and another in college, and then showed me pictures of his grandkids. I swear there were tears in his eyes as he showed me proof of his legacy to this world. This was a guy who had been through the one percenter wars, spent his life defending his club and his country, and was now proud to be a grandpa.

All the one percenters
I spoke to for this book
shared a quiet sense
of gallantry.

I'll tell you something else about one percenters who have spent their lives with their clubs: They're cool, they're calm, and they're genuine. They don't lie and they don't cheat. In other words, they're the kind of men kids can look up to. They shake your hand firmly and with warmth, they look you in the eye, and they don't bullshit you. The fact that they won't take any shit and stand up for what they believe in just makes them all the more attractive and cool because they are the real thing and they are about something.

The way I see it is this: You can live your life proudly, do the right thing, and be about something, or you can be a piece of shit, scared of everything, and be about nothing. Either way, you are gonna die someday. Got that? *You are gonna die!* So you might as well spit in death's face and be about something! Besides, God hates a sniveler.

THE ROAD LESS TRAVELED

In the *One Percenter Code* we have learned that, as human beings, we have a need for a code to live by. This can be seen in all lands, in all times, by every religion ever practiced, by every tribe, group of people, community, or government that has ever existed. There are codes of conduct for organizations, and there are moral codes, from the Ten Commandments of the Judeo/Christian world and the similar commandments of the Koran, to the commandments of Buddhism on down to written rules and laws, and unwritten rules like "don't belch in public."

While basic rules are important to any society, I have to warn you that we must stay constantly alert and watch for laws being passed by our appointed lawmakers that will limit the very freedoms so many Americans have died for. Beware the Patriot Acts of the world, designed to take advantage of our weaknesses and turn us into compliant sheep. These kinds of laws are most often passed when we, as a nation, are at our weakest (like *now*). Those who believe that we need to sacrifice our liberty to obtain protection against the terrorists need take heed of the words of an early one percenter, Benjamin Franklin: "Those who give up some of their liberty in order to obtain a little temporary safety, deserve neither liberty, nor safety." And those who would take our liberty under the guise of providing us safety should take heed of the words of another early one percenter, Thomas Jefferson: "The tree of liberty must be refreshed from time to time with the blood of patriots and tyrants." Got that?

We have seen that the code of bikers takes many of its cues from older, largely unwritten codes, such as the Code of Chivalry of medieval knights, the pirate's code (or articles), and the fabled Code of the West that is still a very real part of the American way of life, as well as the Native American beliefs regarding the respect for all life. As I've shown you, one percenters have real written laws and bylaws for their motorcycle clubs as well as rules of conduct that are known by all bikers, but seldom written down anywhere (until now).

In order to understand basic human growth and the psychology behind how we advance from being creatures bound by fundamental needs to those who are following a spiritual path, we have delved into Maslow's hierarchy of needs and discovered that one cannot move up the pyramid from base needs to grander goals until one is properly motivated. It is also impossible for someone merely in "survival mode" at the bottom of this pyramid to understand the loftier ideals of those who have moved up to having their safety and security needs met.

Every human being has the core need to belong to something and to be accepted by his peers, whether this takes the form of belonging to a company, a sports team, a church, or a motorcycle club. We all seek a family and we all seek to belong. Perhaps this is why so many of our inner-city youth are drawn to street gangs.

I've also shamelessly used this book as a way to instill the concept that you are not your stuff and that the nonsense that

> "Those who give up some of their liberty in order to obtain a little temporary safety, deserve neither liberty, nor safety."

Don't let the fringed jacket fool you; while he might look a little like Dennis Hopper's character from *Easy Rider*, this dude actually knows how to ride his motorcycle.

America has been fed for so long regarding the importance of being a consumer-driven society is a path to ruin. The truth of this is all around us. We are not about what we buy or what we own; we are about who we are inside. In other words, we are the result of our core values and beliefs.

So that you understand where the code of the one percenter came from, I've tried to capture some of the history of the American biker, including the famous Hollister riot (which was far from a riot) that some say started it all, and the resulting letter from the AMA

This kind biker is letting the photographer know that he's number one.

that pointed out that the trouble-making segment of motorcyclists amounts only to "one percent" of riders.

Once you peel away all the stereotypes, media manipulation, and false fear, one percenters are people like you or me or anyone of the over 6 billion bipedal humans on the planet. Though the media has painted a picture of modern-day Vikings or Huns on motorcycles, I've tried to show you the human side of bikers, including the fact that motorcyclists raise more money for charities each year than almost any other group in the world.

In an effort to dig deep into the largely unwritten etiquette of the one percenter, I have interviewed literally hundreds of hardcore bikers and their families to bring you what may be the first-ever compilation of one percenter fact and fiction, rules and laws, ideals and beliefs, and guidelines in the biker world. Remember, when in doubt, show respect!

Over the past 70 years we have seen motorcycle club members go from guys in snappy caps and ties on stock Harleys and Indians to World War II veterans in clubs like the Boozefighters on stripped-down bobbers and to 1970s outlaws on crazy choppers. With the invention of the Evolution motor in the 1980s, doctors and lawyers bought new Harleys by the thousands and the wild ones seemed to turn into the mild ones.

I recently wrote a six-page article for that American standard for old farts, *AARP* magazine, called: "Live Your Motorcycle Fantasy," which explains that millions of baby boomers have succumbed to the romance of the road and that their numbers are growing. According to J.D. Power and Associates, the average age of American bikers jumped from 40 in 2001 to 49 in 2010, and according to the Motorcycle Industry Council, 31 percent of all motorcycle riders are over 50 years old. But the one percenter has lived through it all, showing respect to those who offer respect and surviving by the credo "Live to ride, ride to live."

In a way, this book is sort of like a textbook for rebel school, showing how bikers have passed their code down for generations while instilling courtesy, compassion, and courage among themselves. The one thing that all one percenters have in common is their love for motorcycles; they live, eat, and breathe bikes, and this is a bond that is incredibly strong when shared from father to son (it sure beats video games).

When I was runnin' around on loud motorcycles, jacket flappin' the breeze with a big FTW patch on the back at the tender age of 17, I never would have spent any time thinking about where this long, crazy ride would lead. I sure as hell would not have guessed that the passion for motorcycles would allow me to be the editor of *Easyriders* magazine since 1998, the biker's bible for more than 40 years. In fact, the first issue of *Easyriders* hit the newsstands during my 17th summer and I'll never forget the crazy mix of hippy culture, sex, drugs, and custom choppers that turned my life on its head. I bought that first issue at Rippy's Italian Market in North Miami Beach, Florida, and wondered if I should hide it from my folks. This was before there was full-on nudity in the magazine, but I figured the pro-marijuana point of view and sexy mamas in the rag would probably land me in the principal's office if it were discovered in my locker.

> Perhaps the citizens of
> this country are getting
> fed up with being hand-fed
> bullshit 24 hours a day.

I guess I have always thought of bikers as modern-day cowboys or outlaws and, as such, thought of them as bigger-than-life characters, thanks in part to *Easyriders* magazine. I mean, all you have to do to know that one percenters are bigger than life is to meet one. But I didn't really think about the biker's place in the mythical cosmos. Yet, as Joseph Campbell's work so clearly shows, bikers are archetypical characters, mythic beings that are often used in today's books and movies as antiheroes or reluctant heroes with boots firmly planted along the path of the Hero's Journey.

As important characters in our modern myth, bikers are the living embodiment of a code that transcends common, everyday belief and strives for a way of honor and courage that rivals similar archetypes down through history. We see the biker way in our perception of Viking berserkers, of Native American tribes, of cowboys, of pirates, of Mongols and Huns . . . warrior spirits, all. We see the one percenter iconic spirit in Clint Eastwood's man with no name, in *Star Wars'* reluctant hero Han Solo, and in *Escape from New York's* Snake Plissken. In fact, I believe it is the yearning for strong heroes with backbone and grit that is at the center of America's love affair with the FX series *Sons of Anarchy*. Now more than ever, this country needs characters like Clay Morrow and Jax Teller. Perhaps the citizens of this country are getting fed up with being hand-fed bullshit 24 hours a day.

Just as *Sons of Anarchy* is a bikerized retelling of *Hamlet*, so the sins of the fathers are so often visited upon the sons. As such, I've provided heartfelt life lessons from one percenters, hoping to pass their truth on to future generations. One of my favorites of these tidbits was told to me by a 78-year-old one percenter in a wheelchair who no longer has the use of his legs and is breathing through an oxygen bottle. His advice? "Most of the things you're looking for in life are right in front of you." I could not agree more.

QUESTION EVERYTHING

What can you trust in this world? Trust nothing. Even your senses and your mind can play tricks on you. Rather than trust, I suggest that you question everything. Question everything you have been told. Question everything you have been taught. Question everything you believe. Don't believe what the media is feeding you. Don't believe your government. Don't believe . . . question. This is the difference between rebels and mindless drones. This is the difference between wolves and sheep.

The media- and government-imposed fallacy that the only way to be a happy, prosperous American is to buy stuff you don't need has brought us to the brink of ruin. Our current recession is not over

Today anyone with an understanding loan officer can buy a Harley, but you can't buy the skill needed to ride a chopper down a rough dirt trail.

> Within a few months of a motorcycle club setting up shop in a neighborhood, all the crack dealers and prostitutes move out as the bikers police their territory.

and will not be for some time to come. Our citizens continue to lose their jobs and their homes, our banks are failing, our nation's rating is dropping, and the stock market is a roller coaster ride. College kids are second-guessing their futures, even dropping out of school because they realize that a degree will not guarantee them a job. Young adults are putting off marriage and kids, turning away from buying homes in a market that continues to slide and the great American goal of reaching for the stars is no longer an option.

A recent Gallup poll reveals that fewer than half of Americans believe that the current generation will have a better life than the last generation. Another poll of Americans 18 to 29 found that three-quarters of them expect to delay a major life change or purchase because of economic factors. College kids are second-guessing their majors, realizing that no career path is a safe bet.

Even the few rites of passage that we are allowed in this country have become scams for raking in big bucks by playing on our weaknesses. Ever price out a wedding or a funeral, a baby shower or a divorce? There are all these people (supposed "trained professionals") with their hands out, trying to get you to buy in to the idea that you can't possibly have a funeral without spending $20,000 or a wedding without spending $50,000! While recently going through a divorce, I learned about a new scam called mediation. This is where you pay a so-called professional to write out mediation papers for you and it costs $1,500. That's *before* you see an attorney at $250 per hour.

Even going bankrupt or having a home foreclosed on are money-making scams with attorneys bilking Americans in trouble out of a bunch of money they don't have. Everybody is out to make a buck off of your suffering. So what do we do? How can we turn away from the runaway train that our country has become in favor of a thoughtful, sustainable future? The One Percenter Code shows us that there is another way.

As with all things, you create change one person at a time. When enough people wake up, an interesting thing happens known as the trim tab effect. Giant, ocean-going ships have massive rudders that turn the ships, but those rudders need help. A small trim tab is a rudder within the rudder. The small trim tab turns the bigger rudder that then turns the giant ship. Change is like that. Margaret Mead said, "Never doubt that a small group of thoughtful people can change the world. Indeed, it's the only thing that ever has."

One percenter motorcycle clubs have often gone into the worst neighborhoods in a city and opened a clubhouse there. Within a few months all the crack dealers and prostitutes move out as the bikers police their territory. Before long, the neighborhood starts to revive. Every year bikers from small towns all over America show us that a small group can have a major impact by raising millions of dollars for charities, giving blood, raising barns, whatever it takes. Rebels or not, they are an active part of their communities.

The answer for America is not to become bigger and add more red tape to our overtaxed system. The answer is to act locally. Start in your own community and make a difference. We will win back our country one block at a time. If I make it sound as though America is at war with itself, it is! In a time in which many of us don't know our neighbors and never speak to people as we walk our city streets, the time has come to embrace what we truly love about our country: our humanity.

Go out and meet your neighbors; hell, have a block party! Walk down the street of your town and talk to people. Be a human! Talk to a homeless person and find out his or her story. People without homes are just like you and me. Most of us are just one paycheck away from joining them on the streets anyway. You may also meet a few of the growing numbers of young people who *choose* to be homeless or "homefree," who turn their backs on the system completely. You can also buy locally. Buy produce from local farms, become part of a local co-op, support local business instead of selling your soul to Walmart.

ONE FINAL RANT!

This is not the America I thought I would grow up in. It is uptight and judgmental, so religiously twisted and bent out about sex that pornography runs rampant, so confused about our purpose in the world that we pretend to be the planet's peacekeepers while murdering innocents every day, so screwed financially that we are fast becoming the world's biggest third-world country. And I am sick of being lied to and preached to by people I don't respect. I'm sick of cell phone–gabbing zombies running over bikers because they weren't paying attention. I've had it with insane laws and litigation where old ladies make millions because the coffee they were served was so hot they got burned and then they sued the restaurant, or the cops who have to enforce city vending laws against kids selling lemonade in front of their houses. I'm sick of intellectual snobs who think they have all the answers. I'm fed up with an entire generation that is so devoid of real emotions that they can only text cute, meaningless bullshit (LOL) instead of having a heart-to-heart conversation with a real human being. Yep, I'm fed up.

But you know what? It is still my country and I still tear up on the Fourth of July when they play the national anthem. I'll bet many of you reading this feel the same way. The One Percenter Code teaches us that a small, dedicated group can make a difference. It teaches us that we are all individuals, and it is the honoring of our differences and our individuality that makes this country great.

Our Declaration of Independence includes the following: "We hold these truths to be self-evident, that all men are created equal,

> The One Percenter Code teaches us that a small, dedicated group can make a difference.

that they are endowed by their Creator with certain unalienable rights, that among these are life, liberty and the pursuit of happiness." Please understand that the pursuit of happiness is not the pursuit of stuff as we have been led to believe. Rather it is the honest pursuit of a life free of oppression. We have become slaves to consumerism, worshiping a false god.

One percenters don't buy into the promise that shopping is the answer. It is time to let go of the consumer-driven society concept and become human again. Did you know that some of the most content people in the world are also some of the poorest? The United Kingdom's *Guardian* website named Nigeria as having the happiest citizens, even though the country is plagued by poverty, corruption, and violence. A recent poll named Nigeria as the world's most optimistic nation. According to the article:

> In a 53-country Gallup poll, Nigerians were rated at 70 points for optimism. By contrast, Britain scored a deeply pessimistic -44. What makes Nigerians so happy? At first glance it's hard to see: Nigeria is seen as a place where corruption thrives. The newspapers are filled with sensational allegations of crooked officials and mind-boggling hauls—the former CEO of Oceanic Bank, Cecilia Ibru, is said to be just one of the worst. Sectarian violence is steadily on the up, most recently with the Christmas Eve bombs in the northern city of Jos. Nor are Nigerians strangers to civil war and unrest, the most terrible being the three-year Biafran war. Then there is the grinding poverty.
>
> But look harder and the optimism seems less misplaced. Nigeria has the third-largest economy in Africa—and it's still growing. There's the oft-repeated statistic that one in every six Africans is Nigerian. The UN estimates the population at 154,729,000—astonishing for a nation about twice the size of California.
>
> Daily life is hardly one glorious Technicolor dance sequence, but I have never lived in such a happy place. I can't give a definite answer, but I think the joy comes from seeing and living through the worst that life can offer; it is an optimism born of hope.
>
> There's a spirit of entrepreneurship—people seem bewildered if you admit a lack of ambition. Nigerians want to go places and believe—rightly or wrongly—that they can. That drive and

ambition fuels their optimism; they're working towards happiness, so they're happy.

This goes back to my belief that you control your life and create your own reality, one moment at a time. If you don't like your life, change it. You have the ability each day to have a glorious day, each moment at a time . . . or not. You choose. Of all the self-help books ever written, it really is as simple as this: *You* make it all happen.

Ask yourself this question: How good do I dare make my life? How good can you stand it?

* * *

In this book I've written a great deal about what other bikers think and how they go through life, what's important to them, and how they live the One Percenter Code each and every day. Now it's my turn. Sometimes things happen to you that you would never expect to happen while travelin' down the road of life. You know that old saying "That which does not kill you, makes you stronger"? It turns out to be true after all.

In my 57 years of life I've had my share of ups and downs, just like everybody. I've lost my grandparents, my parents, and most of my relatives but never lost faith in God. I went to jail for something I didn't do (don't they all say that?), but I never lost my belief in justice. I've been married and divorced three times but never lost love. I've lost jobs but never lost hope.

During this last year while writing this book, one month was particularly challenging: I found out that my wife of 15 years wanted to divorce me and that the only way to provide child and spousal support would be for me to go bankrupt and possibly lose my house. I had all four of my wisdom teeth taken out and had skin cancer removed from my face and all this in the same month. I guess when it rains, it pours.

Through all this adversity, I just kept thinking how lucky I am, how blessed and fortunate that I have no real problems. I am grateful every day. My ex-wife has stayed my best friend, my son is still in my life, and I can look into his eyes and ask him what he's thinking about. My other family, my close friends, and the editors and crew

Today, as the general public becomes increasingly aware of the contributions bikers make to society, more and more of them are being welcomed into communities all across the country. That wasn't always the case.

at Paisano Publications, have kept me on the path, fed me, given me moral and spiritual support as well as Cadillac margaritas and a lot of laughter. It also really hit home with me that we are not our stuff. All that stuff you have worked so hard to buy is meaningless. Wouldn't you trade it all for just one more day of life . . . to watch one more sunset?

I have to say that the beliefs and practices of the One Percenter Code have kept me afloat while cast adrift on perilous seas. Walking the walk is easy when nothing is pushing you down. I learned that you never really know who you are until you experience some adversity in this life. It's not what happens to you that determines who you are; it's what you do with what happens to you.

Keep to the Code,
Dave Nichols

INDEX

ONE PERCENTER TITLES

One Percenter
The Legend of
the Outlaw Biker
ISBN: 9780760338292

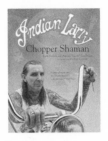

Indian Larry
Chopper Shaman
ISBN: 9780760338278

Riding on the Edge
A Motorcycle
Outlaw's Tale
ISBN: 9780760341339

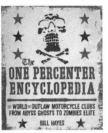

The One Percenter
Encyclopedia
From Abyss Ghosts
to Zombies Elite
ISBN: 9780760341100

Terry the Tramp
The Life and
Dangerous Times
of a One Percenter
ISBN: 9780760340059

The Original
Wild Ones
Tales of the
Boozefighters
Motorcycle Club
ISBN: 9780760335376

Biker's Handbook
Becoming Part of the
Motorcycle Culture
ISBN: 9780760332108